EX LIBRIS

BANANARAMA

Really Saying Something

SARA DALLIN & KEREN WOODWARD

HUTCHINSON
LONDON

1 3 5 7 9 10 8 6 4 2

Hutchinson
20 Vauxhall Bridge Road
London SW1V 2SA

Hutchinson is part of the Penguin Random House group of companies
whose addresses can be found at global.penguinrandomhouse.com

Penguin
Random House
UK

First published in the United Kingdom by Hutchinson in 2020

www.penguin.co.uk

A CIP catalogue record for this book is available from the British Library.

ISBN 9781786332660 (Hardcover)
ISBN 9781786332844 (Trade Paperback)

Plate sections designed by Dinah Drazin

Typeset in 11.75/16.5 pt ITC Stone Serif by Jouve (UK), Milton Keynes
Printed and bound in Great Britain by Clays Ltd, Elcograf S.p.A.

Penguin Random House is committed to a sustainable future for our
business, our readers and our planet. This book is made from
Forest Stewardship Council® certified paper.

This memoir is dedicated to
Tom and Alice,
our precious children

CONTENTS

CONTENTS

PROLOGUE

31 May 1989

SARA: It was the most fun we could have imagined, our 1989 world tour. A fast and furious set of wall-to-wall hits; it was a triumph. Now we were about to take to the stage for one of our final shows – at Wembley Arena.

We'd kicked off in America, three months earlier, followed by Asia and Australia. Now we were on home turf, with our family, friends and fans eagerly waiting in the audience. In the dressing room, costumes hung on rails and make-up lay on tables, while our routine warm-up music – Kate Bush and The Smiths – played on the boom box. As the start of the show approached, we were led by torchlight into the darkness under the stage, ready to burst through the shiny, black lacquered floor on a hydraulic lift.

The moment grew closer. The audience sensed something was about to happen and the roar and thumping of feet on the floor grew deafening. It was electric. As I climbed into the cramped space, preparing

1

for our ascent, I could feel my heart racing, the adrenaline pumping. We giggled as we adjusted our limbs to give ourselves more room. The lights dimmed, the band made their way onto the stage and the dancers took up their positions, prompting an almighty roar. I looked over at Keren and thought, *I used to sit next to you in French at school. How did we get here?* As quick as the thought came, we were on the move, rising like goddesses through the darkness into dazzling spotlights.

Bananarama. The pop stars.

I

SIXTIES BABIES

SARA: As a child, I was a constant daydreamer; always lost in some fantasy. On my first trip to the theatre, we saw *Peter Pan*. I'll never forget seeing him fly through a sparkling night sky and desperately wanting to be one of the Darling children.

I was mesmerised by the stories I learned in Sunday school – the Technicolor pictures in my Bible of people from faraway lands, bathed in halos of light, where Jesus miraculously fed 5,000 people from five loaves and two fishes, turned water into wine and helped lame people walk. I always wondered how he did that.

Spurred on by the thought of these superpowers, I decided to try a little magic of my own. One Sunday morning I took an egg from the fridge, wrapped it in a tissue and held it against the radiator, waiting for it to hatch. It didn't, of course, and the terrible mess left me thoroughly deflated.

I loved the escapism of movies and looked forward to the Saturday cinema trips with my siblings and our school friends. We were dropped off outside the ABC, each with a tube of Rowntree's Fruit Pastilles or Spangles, ready for a morning of children's movies and cartoons. There was once a mad man loose in the cinema, screaming and frothing at the mouth. I have no idea how he got in as it was meant to be strictly children only. It was absolutely terrifying and I remember we all ducked down in our little red velvet seats.

Every Saturday afternoon, my family and I would visit my grannie's for tea; something I always looked forward to. She'd buy us sweets and comics: Curly Wurlys, Crunchies and *Twinkle* magazine for me. This was before I progressed to *Jackie* magazine a few years later, leading to my discovery of the pin-up pop stars of the day. On arrival, we'd rush through the little passageway tunnel that separated the terraced houses, into her beautiful little rose garden. At the end of the garden were gooseberry bushes and a large concrete air raid shelter that no one was allowed to enter so my siblings and I – along with the neighbour's grandchildren – all climbed on the roof to play. Having no concept of war or German bombers, we all imagined how exciting it would be to sleep inside there wrapped in cosy blankets, eating jam on toast by candlelight. There was always an old black-and-white Hollywood film to watch in the afternoon, starring Errol Flynn, Gene Kelly, Bette Davis or Judy Garland, with plenty of singing, dancing and swashbuckling. Then it would be the wrestling, football results and finally our favourite shows: *Doctor Who*, *Dad's Army* and *The Generation Game*.

I loved the escapism of the movies, the glamour of Hollywood . . . but it all seemed so far away. That was until a few years later when some research into our family tree threw up some French aristocratic roots, along with an impressive family crest and some Irish ancestry. The discovery that my relatives in Boston, USA, had often played golf with the Kennedys, somehow brought all that glamour a little closer to home. My Uncle Lee was a professor at Harvard and he and my Auntie Mavis would come over to England to visit. My auntie always looked like a movie star, right down to the Bette Davis-style cigarette holder. She'd waft in smelling of Chanel No. 5 with her glamorous clothes and she'd sing us songs and tell us all about her exciting travels. When it was time for them to leave, we'd all go to a rooftop at the airport and watch the plane take off. I remember looking at the little round plane windows with the tiny people looking out, and watching as it accelerated down the runway and disappeared into the sky. It was the most exciting thing I'd ever seen and I wished I could fly too.

With the absence of computers the only real access to information was at the library and it's where I went to discover new worlds. My mother had taught me, my brother and my sister to read before we started school – we'd worked our way through the *Janet and John* books and later my favourites *Topsy and Tim* and *The Moomins*.

It's hard to explain the thrill of my weekly visit there as a small child with my father and younger sister Lindsey, planning which books I might take out, praying I wouldn't have to be put on the waiting list. In winter, I'd crunch

Sara's mum and her Uncle Neil bidding a fond farewell to their sister
Mavis before she jets back to America. Neil's fiancée, Sylvia, is far left.

through the snow, in my red wellies and homemade cape.
The snow was never deep enough to look beautiful and
was usually a dirty brown colour from the muddy puddles
beneath. But in springtime, the path was strewn with
blossom, blown from the trees, reminding me of the
confetti my sister and I collected in our pockets from the
nearby churchyard after weddings. The library had a
couple of little tables where I could sit and feel tremen-
dously grown-up, but most of the time I preferred to
sprawl on the lovely old polished floors with my pile of
books. The sunlight streamed through the windows and I
would lie like a cat, soaking up the sunshine. The smell of
polished wood always takes me back to that happy place.

My first memory of Keren was seeing her in the playground at maybe four or five years old. Her nickname was Jumping Jellybean but I've always called her Woody. We weren't in the same class at school so weren't friends right away. Her best friend was Gina and mine was Jenny, who was tall and willowy with long blond hair, blue eyes and very pretty. Sadly, Jenny moved to South Africa. Then there was Claire, who also left, followed by Susan. Each loss felt devastating as I'd have to start all over again with someone new. Fortunately, Julie Driscoll stuck around.

Eventually, when we were about seven, Keren and I became friends. She had shiny, poker-straight hair, which she wore in bunches with cola-cube hair bobbles and a gold slide at the side. Keren's mother made clothes in her spare time, so she had an endless supply of gorgeous mini dresses. I didn't have quite as many, but my favourite was a purply blue dress from C&A with elasticated ruching at the waist. I loved a mini dress with white knee-length socks – and as we got older, we were forever hiking our school skirts and summer dresses up with the help of a snake belt. The American tan tight, worn under white knee-length socks, was also a popular look at junior school in the seventies, giving a sun-kissed look to a winter leg. Unless you were one of the fortunate who got to spend a week in Majorca on a package holiday, it was the only way you were ever going to look like you had a tan in Blighty. I have a clear memory of walking to school and my mum stopping to chat to 'Auntie' Mary, our neighbour. I was transfixed by the long, dark hairs that were crushed and very clearly visible under those same tan tights. Most unsavoury.

—

KEREN: All of my clothes were homemade. Mostly out of Crimplene, which was the Lycra of its day. It didn't fray and had a little give, so it was quite user-friendly. I had a ridiculous number of incredibly short dresses, most of which had patch pockets, mandarin collars and zips up the front. For playing, I also had minuscule shorts and hot pants with bibs. My best friend Gina and I had matching trouser suits with waistcoats fastened by chains, which we wore with high-collar blouses with layers of frill at the neck like a couple of faux Georgian dandies.

Of course, all I ever really wanted was something that came from a real shop, rather than something Mum had knocked up. Even my Brownie uniform was homemade, and I hated it because it wasn't the same as all the other girls'. I didn't have an armful of badges, and could never be bothered with bob-a-job week. But I was the Sixer in the Elves and responsible for collecting the subs, although the thrupenny bits I collected sometimes made their way into my pocket rather than Brown Owl's, where they were used to buy sweets.

Despite my disdain for an exclusively handmade wardrobe, the sewing skills I learned from Mum came in handy down the line when wide flares were in fashion. She took me to the market where we'd buy yards of Trevira, and together we would fashion the widest flares with the biggest waistbands at a fraction of the cost of the shop-bought equivalent. We did most of our sewing while watching old films and musicals on TV; one of us would spread the patterns out on the floor, while the other would sit at the machine, like a production line. My grandma's green 1960s Hammerite Singer sewing machine ended up coming to London with me, and we ran up a fair few of the early Bananarama outfits on it, all with fabrics we bought from the market in Leather Lane. I still have that sewing machine, and I still use it.

When Sara and I first became friends, I was envious of her thick, wavy hair, which she wore in a high ponytail, tied with a ribbon. I, meanwhile, had thin, straight hair which my mother always tried to disguise by putting curlers in it. It's no different today, a fact that numerous hairdressers have discovered an hour into any photo or video shoot, when, despite any number of

Clip-on hairpiece providing much needed volume at Auntie Meg and Uncle Joe's wedding.

expensive products, my hair's deathly straightness returns, with the added bonus of the aforementioned products turning it into something that resembles a sheaf of straw. For most of my young childhood, I wore my hair in bunches and was the proud owner of an excellent selection of bobbles and hair slides. I fastened the bunches over my ears, convinced they were massive and stuck out. But now I think this was just an illusion, caused by my dangerously thin hair.

I met Sara at infants' school. We were in different classes but lived within a few streets of each other. Sara was sporty, as was I, and along with our friends, we played 'Bulldog', 'Off Ground Touch' and, occasionally, kiss chase in the playground. During the latter, Sara would invariably end up being caught by her 'boyfriend' Michael, who I considered to be the most handsome boy in the school. My crush of the day, meanwhile, was my tall, dark and handsome class teacher, who had the best lamb-chop sideburns a girl could dream of. We also loved French elastic, skipping and a strange pastime that involved swinging a ball in a pair of tights (American Tan obviously) against a wall, and under our kicking legs.

We were both musical and sang in the school choir, which was run by Sara's teacher. I'd been learning the piano from the age of four, and also sang in a choir called The Maytones, who performed concerts in churches. In The Maytones, we all wore kingfisher-blue dresses with gold trim at the neck, and I always sang the descant harmonies. We finished each concert with a rousing rendition of the 'Hallelujah Chorus' from Handel's

Messiah. The choir was run by a very formidable, hefty woman who also taught me the piano. She had a deep voice like the actress Peggy Mount and used it to great effect. Any mistakes were met with a rap on the knuckles and a deafening reprimand. She used a walking frame and during one piano lesson shuffled out of the room to go to the bathroom. A few minutes later I heard her bellow my name, so I jumped to attention and ran to her, thinking she'd had a fall. Instead, she asked me to help her pull up the most colossal, flesh-coloured bloomers, the likes of which might have been worn by Hattie Jacques in a *Carry On* film. You could have run them up a flagpole and seen them for miles. I was so traumatised, I left the lesson in tears and begged Mum to let me stop going, to no avail.

Perhaps it was because Mum was the unmusical child of a very talented family that she was so determined I should persevere. My grandfather was an incredible pianist, and I particularly loved listening to him play dramatic Rachmaninov pieces. Mum's two sisters played too, and my Auntie Meg took a degree in music and ended up as head of music at my school. Family get-togethers involved my cousins and I sharing the piano stool, banging out show tunes or hymns while everyone sang along. If you didn't bag a place on the stool you were lumbered with playing along on the recorder.

I loved taking part in piano Eisteddfods, especially coming away with a certificate or a medal, but I hated singing on my own in public. I'd get so nervous, I'd get a nosebleed at the very thought of it. Unfortunately, at one school Christmas concert, I was picked to sing 'In the Bleak Midwinter' as a solo, which terrified the life out of me to the point where I almost wet myself.

—

SARA: Auditioning for the school choir, aged seven, was an enormous deal. It was so competitive, and the idea of not getting in and being excluded was terrifying. Everyone queued up outside the classroom and, one by one, took their place next to the music teacher at the piano, who would strike up the opening chords to 'There Is a Green Hill Far Away'. And, just like on *The X Factor*, each auditionee was either given a chair or sent packing. It was with great relief that both Keren and I were offered places. The stage for the choir's performances was three-tiered and made up of gym blocks. Keren and I were the smallest, so were always positioned on the top tier right in the middle. There we'd stand in our little home-knitted cardigans and miniskirts: Keren's hair in bunches, and mine in a ponytail with a carefully selected ribbon from my collection. At one Christmas performance, Keren accepted a solo verse in 'Hark! the Herald Angels Sing', which I thought very brave. I had enough to concentrate on with the extra burden of the tedious classical pieces I had to play on the recorder.

My memory is that we were quite an impressive choir, and my favourite part was learning the harmonies in groups and then putting them all together. We learned how to build a song, the crescendo, the Italian names for loud – *forte* – and very soft – *pianissimo* – and how to follow the conductor. We also learned to read and write music and played in the school band, where the songs were usually bizarre and always religious. Songs about Daniel in the lions' den, and the 'Cowboy Carol', whose lyrics are etched into my brain. I was never sure if they were about Jesus or a more earthbound romance. At one point, Keren and I were given a solo spot at one of the concerts, playing xylophones. I was very anxious about not having enough rehearsal time and told my form teacher who was in charge of the show that I didn't want to do it. He was very encouraging, telling me I'd be great and not to give up. Determined not to let him or myself down I went home and built a xylophone from Lego, Sellotaping the notes to the bricks, so I could practise away. The resulting performance was, to my relief, perfect!

I would probably have enjoyed the music side of things much more had my music teacher not been so brutal, she was unbearably strict. One day, in a non-music-related 'show and tell' class, a girl brought in a giant tomato her grandfather had grown. During break, a classmate threw it on the floor, smashing it into a squelched mess. She then told the music teacher that I'd perpetrated the crime, and – despite quietly protesting that it wasn't me – I got my legs slapped hard. I think I was about seven or eight years old at the time and since then I have always been sensitive to injustice.

One of Keren's and my earliest escapades was trying to break each other's ankles by taking it in turns to throw bricks at them. We'd noticed how much attention kids got when they came into school with a broken arm or leg. Teachers would fuss over them, and classmates were desperate to sign their plaster casts. This was something we needed to experience. Hoping to garner some of that extra attention for ourselves, we headed to the park. The plan was that we'd break our ankles, be whisked off to hospital by lunchtime, and return home before *Blue Peter* with the ultimate attention-grabbing accessory – a pair of crutches. When this proved unsuccessful we realised we'd just have to find other ways of getting noticed.

I seemed to spend a great deal of my early childhood running. Running to Keren's house to see if she could come out to play, running to the park, running through the 'snake field', running home at dusk. I had an inordinate amount of energy. I was super sporty, and much happier in shorts and a T-shirt than I was in dresses. I loved my dolls and dressing up but I was also a bit of a tomboy, always on at my brother Paul to let me play football with him and his friends. I climbed trees, and built spaceships with the neighbours' boys, Andrew and Ian, and my sister Lindsey. We had so much fun just in the garden building things with old bits of carpet, planks of wood and discarded doors from kitchen units.

Keren and I would cycle to a local river, dash the bikes to the ground, roll our jeans up over our knees and wade upstream in our black school plimsolls, wanting to see how far we could go without getting our clothes wet or being swept away. On one occasion, after climbing out of the river, we took off our shoes to empty the water, both screaming in unison. Keren had acquired a stickleback in her plimsoll.

Sometimes, we'd fish in the river, with flimsy nets attached to bamboo canes, or pick crab apples from the trees to stuff in our saddle bags. We didn't realise that you weren't supposed to eat them, until we ended up with terrible stomach aches.

I loved family day trips to castles and stately homes, but especially trips to the seaside with donkeys and sand dunes. I remember once getting a free plastic kite from the Texaco petrol station on the way and waiting excitedly for my dad to tie the string to it so it could fly. It repeatedly nosedived into the sand dunes, only ever managing to stay airborne for four seconds. Often these days out involved my dad shouting words of encouragement at the car, desperately hoping it wouldn't break down as it shuddered up a steep hill. My mum would break out Tupperware boxes of cheese sandwiches and homemade fairy cakes as the three of us bleated, 'Are we there yet? Can you see the sea?' from the back seat, the age-old cry of many a bored, travelling child. Poor Lindsey, the smallest of us, was always trapped in the middle, unable to see out and feeling very car sick while my brother Paul and I hogged the windows, singing along to Dave Dee, Dozy, Beaky, Mick and Tich's classic hit 'The Legend of Xanadu'.

These were the simplest of times and the happiest memories.

The local park was a permanent social fixture for us as kids. We'd tear down there after school and bag our place on the steam roller, which, now I think about it, as it had gears and a brake, was probably an actual piece of machinery that someone had left there. Once we were in the driving seat there was no moving us and a queue would form until eventually we got bored and climbed down.

I loved the long summer evenings and the smell when the grass had been freshly cut. On those evenings, we would stay out until the light started to fade, hiding behind the small grassy hill near the swings while we awaited the inevitable arrival of one of our dads to chaperone us home. Sometimes, if it was misty, we'd see the silhouette of one of them approach through the huge blue metal gates, scanning the park to look for us. We'd try to stay hidden as long as we could, thinking it was hilarious fun.

With our friends, we played a peculiar game in front of the park pavilion with a stick of chalk, or a stone if we didn't have that. We drew squares on the ground and asked four questions, then we'd fill in the answers with the chalk.

'What age will you get married?'

'What will his name be?'

'How many children will you have?'

'How many boys, how many girls?'

My answers were always the same. He'd be called Michael; I'd marry between sixteen and seventeen, and have four or five children, more boys than girls or maybe two of each.

We took it in turns to chalk out our answers, and if a girl wrote that she'd be married at nineteen, we'd all say, 'Oh no! That's really old.' As it turned out, my answers were very wide of the mark, as were Keren's.

Keren and I became even closer once we moved to senior school. We passed the entrance exam to the local grammar school, but after a few years it morphed into a comprehensive. For the most part, my school days were really enjoyable, except for a brief spell of bullying when I started there at eleven. A handful of third-year girls, aged fourteen, decided to pick on me for no reason I could fathom. These were the same girls who got 'blind drunk' at the school disco and I took that literally and had nightmares for the next week. They shouted insults as I passed through classrooms for the change of lessons and the bullying culminated with them locking me in the girls' changing rooms so that I missed my lunch while I could hear them saying my name and laughing outside. The fear of seeing these girls on the stairs or in the corridors was blood-draining. It didn't last all that long, although it seemed like an eternity to me then. The strange thing was I never told anybody; I just suffered in silence.

Early teens can be a vile time for girls. Back then, it was all about who was cool and who wasn't; who had new clothes and who didn't. Keren and I were both party to, and victims of, this girl-group mentality. The group we hung around with were the cool clique and everything was fine until Jackie, who was supposedly my best friend at the time, decided that I wasn't welcome in the group any more. One weekend, Keren and the rest of the girls went to her house for a sleepover, leaving me feeling horribly left out. Looking back, I'm not sure I was missing out on all that much. They ended up sleeping in a small coal cellar under the house and eating Arctic roll in their sleeping bags. It was hardly the Bloomsbury set.

Eventually, I was back in favour, but then it was Keren's turn to be ostracised. Her isolation lasted the whole of the summer holidays, so she missed out on local youth club nights and church hall discos. By the end of that summer, I was getting bored with the group. They only wanted to hang around the park, watching the boys play football, which wasn't exactly my idea of fun. So, after school one day, I went to Keren's house, unannounced, to ask if she wanted to hang out.

Of course, there was much contemplation about what might happen if the other girls found out we'd teamed up, but ultimately, we decided we didn't care. We had missed one another's company and realised that we had much more in common with each other than we did with the other girls. Deciding we didn't need anyone else, we pricked our fingers with a compass, swearing an oath to be best friends for ever.

—

KEREN: Outside of the gang, I really didn't have much confidence. Apparently, my exclusion from the group occurred due to me being a) too small, and b) too spoilt, because I had a monthly clothing allowance, amounting to £10. It was horrible being made to feel like an outcast at that age, just because I was a late developer. I cried a lot, convinced I was a short-arsed freak who would never need a bra. I spent the best part of that summer holiday wondering what on earth to do with myself.

When Sara turned up at my door to float the idea of us going to the Radio 1 Roadshow, I was over the moon. Radio 1 Roadshows were a huge deal at the time. Various disc jockeys – like Noel Edmonds, Dave Lee Travis or Simon Bates – would visit coastal towns across the country to broadcast a live set and meet local people who'd take part in games and quizzes. Travelling to that first roadshow involved a bus and then a couple of trains, where we danced between the carriages to the rhythm of the engine, accompanied by an hysterical old lady with whiskers and a twitch. It was one of our earliest adventures, of which there would later be many.

After that we started hanging around at one another's houses regularly, listening to music. I recall feeling mortified when Sara came to call for me and my mum wouldn't let me out until I had finished my piano practice. What must she have thought? Particularly as I was wearing the white crocheted trousers that Mum had made me.

—

I'd been given a Waltham cassette recorder as a birthday present and I recorded the Top Twenty every Sunday. I'd then take it to my room so I could listen again to my personal favourites. At the same time, my dad danced around, whistling to *Sing Something Simple* with Cliff Adams, which was on directly after the chart rundown.

The first big crush Sara and I shared was David Essex, and his face adorned my bedroom wall. There were definite camps among the girls in my class, with some obsessing over Donny Osmond, who was a bit too goody-two shoes for me, as was David Cassidy.

It was the 1970s, and the music we really loved came from glam rock artists, like The Sweet and T. Rex. Once we discovered Bowie and Roxy Music, there was no looking back. Sara's living room was the perfect place for practising our choreography because it had parquet flooring, just like a real dance floor. Sometimes, we'd forget the routines and just slide around with cushion covers on our feet; then the cushion covers would become hats, and we'd use rolls of wallpaper, or whatever other props we could find, as guitars. My house, on the other hand, had recently been modernised and was now quite magnificently 1970s, boasting an orange and brown kitchen with wallpaper that clashed horribly. The hall carpet was orange and green, on which sat a telephone table with built-in seat and space for the phone book, with a mustard-coloured plastic telephone on top.

Post-modernisation of the house, Mum decided the Victorian upright piano had to go because it didn't fit in with the swirling brown and cream carpet and plush, coffee-coloured Dralon three-piece suite. To be honest, I'm not sure anything would have. On this topic, I wasn't consulted. The piano was just removed. Now, if I wanted to practise, I had to go to my grandma's house and play my Auntie Meg's baby grand. By then, Auntie Meg had taken over from my dragon of a piano teacher, and continued to coach me through all of my piano exams and my music O-level. I eventually inherited that piano, but I'm ashamed to say it's a little out of tune as I rarely play it. I like to think that one day I'll brush up the piano skills I let slide.

Our living room was only used when we had visitors, but it contained the best thing in the whole house, which was a record player. My parents went out to a dance at the local rugby club most Saturdays, so my brother Matt and I had the place to ourselves. Sara would come over, and my brother would usually have a friend over too. We played music and got up to no good.

Thinking about it, I'm not sure we were old enough to be left unsupervised, and there were often complaints from the neighbours about the noise. The grumpy man next door, who we called Rock John, would take his revenge by mowing his lawn with a thunderous motor mower at the crack of dawn on a Sunday when we were having a lie-in. This led to a war between us, culminating in my brother Matt shooting him in the arse with his air rifle from the bedroom window, like some sort of sniper assassin. While Rock John had no concrete evidence as to who fired the rifle, the police were nonetheless called. Luckily, my ever-pragmatic mum was able to get Matt off the hook by telling the attending officers that her son's biggest dream was to follow in his uncle's footsteps and become a policeman. She assured them that he'd never jeopardise his goal by doing anything as reckless as firing an air rifle out of an upstairs window.

—

SARA: We'd get together most nights and weekends, taping songs from the radio, plugging a little mic into

Keren's tape recorder, and singing over the top. We learned every lyric and backing vocal to our chosen songs and even worked out all the harmonies before we put the vocals down. 'The Bangin' Man' by Slade, 'Ben' by Michael Jackson and 'Evergreen' by Barbra Streisand were early favourites. We loved the complicated and intricate harmonies of Simon and Garfunkel's 'Bridge Over Troubled Water'. Whenever Keren's parents were out, we'd sprawl on the floor in her living room, surrounded by record covers, while we learned lyrics and read every album cover note. As it got dark, the street lamp outside the house would bathe the room in an orangey glow which made the experience, and the music, seem even more magical. If we weren't learning lyrics or singing, we were making up dance routines on Keren's landing. Sylvester's 'You Make Me Feel (Mighty Real)' was the standout routine of the time. Unfortunately, my choreographical over-enthusiasm led to the obliteration of a vase, which had been a wedding present for Keren's parents. We blamed her brother and his football for that one.

—

KEREN: Though we didn't succeed in breaking our ankles, we endured lots of injuries later. Many of them happened while out on our bikes, which played a significant part in our lives. We had once both been proud owners of the Moulton Mini before I graduated to a blue and red, big-wheeled Raleigh. In truth, I'd have preferred a Chopper, but those were beyond Mum and Dad's budget. Mudguards were customarily removed as that was the in-thing to do, as was pegging cards onto the wheel spokes, so the faster you went, the louder the clacking. If ever it was raining, dirty water sprayed up the back of our matching fluffy, cream bomber jackets, from Etam, which we usually teamed with burgundy brushed-denim flares with white zips. One of my favourite looks, for sure.

Cycling home from the park one evening, I discovered that if you tossed your head around wildly, from side to side, it put a whole new slant on the biking experience. On my say-so, Sara was keen to give it a go, but her over-enthusiastic head tossing caused her to career into a brick wall and sail over the handlebars into a flowerbed. Other injuries were more routine: flapping flares were always liable to get caught in the bike chain, which could be especially painful when you were giving your best friend a 'backie', and the brute force of her slamming into you on a sharp stop propelled you into, or over, the handlebars.

When the fair came to town, we loved to cycle there. I adored the lights and music, with each ride playing the chart hits of the day, including all the cheesy ones – songs by Kenny and Pilot. We screamed our way round the Waltzer and, of course, the more you screamed, the more the young men would spin you. The Octopus was the same, but, hating heights, I never really enjoyed the big wheel. Occasionally, I'd end up getting on it with some evil child, who would swing us about wildly while we dangled at the top.

—

SARA: It was such a thrill when the fairground boys would let us have a free Waltzer ride. We'd all cram into the car giggling, singing along to the strains of Billy Ocean's 'Red Light Spells Danger', and I remember the disappointment I felt when proceedings were brought to an abrupt end because someone had vomited during the opening chords of Shirley and Company's 'Shame, Shame, Shame'. I also remember the smell of hot dogs and candy floss, the shouts and the laughter, the music and the flashing lights – all part of our youth. Keren and I would hang around the rides listening to the music, chatting with our friends, in our homemade extra-wide flares with patch pockets, our cap-sleeved T-shirts and feather cuts and no money in our pockets. Then we'd hop on our bikes and ride home.

—

KEREN: We escaped to the local park whenever we could, hanging out on the swings or climbing frame, or the wooden shelter at the top of the slide. When it rained, we'd while away the hours in a concrete pipe, which might not sound all that interesting, but we were never bored. Sara and I had wild imaginations and put them to good use writing sketches and making up plays, which invariably transferred to the roof of the park pavilion. This might sound grand but was, in truth, a concrete block with a reception desk, changing rooms and toilets. It was run by a park keeper who, we suspected, had a penchant for the young boys he coached at football. My brother Matt and his friends used to race out of the showers in fear of being caught by him and held on his lap. We used to lean over the roof and throw berries at him for amusement, and he'd come running out angrily, with no idea where they were coming from. We never told our parents about our suspicions but someone must have said something, because he ended up in prison.

A fair amount of snogging with local boys went on in that park at the weekends, particularly in the den in the snake field, which was a hollowed-out pit in the middle of a scrubby field full of brambles. The den had a roof of corrugated iron, which was weighed down with planks of wood, and the inside was lined with old bits of carpet. We'd illuminate it with candles and spend hours in there. On one long, hot afternoon, our friend Gina lit a small fire to see how long she dared to leave it before stamping it out. It was, of course, inevitable that it would burn wildly out of control, sending us all into a panic and running away. A local neighbour called the fire brigade, but Gina had been spotted. Incredibly, she actually went home and told her mum, who didn't seem to think it was that big a deal. I can only imagine the trouble I'd have been in if I'd done the same. At the very least I would have heard my mum's favourite catch-phrase, 'Wait until your father gets home', and it would probably have resulted in a light slippering.

—

SARA: We were always looking for a chance to shine and, while the school orchestra really wasn't that great, our annual school musicals were magnificent. In *Annie*

Get Your Gun, Keren and I played one of several Native American Indians. Our costumes were rough, hessian sacks which we were instructed to cut holes in, for arms, and decorate with a Native American design – whatever that was.

South Pacific was slightly higher end as far as the costume department went: grass skirts and bikini tops adorned with flowers. Keren and I were singled out to stand in front of the gauze curtain at the start of the show, separating us from our classmates. They were merely regular natives and hidden behind the gauze. Being featured in this way meant that we were given much more glamorous make-up, and flowers in our hair. Our final musical was *Guys and Dolls*, which was a much more

Our magnificent school play, *South Pacific*.

26

raucous affair with boys from the local sixth form taking the Marlon Brando and Frank Sinatra parts. In this production, Keren and I were the Hot Box Girls, singing in a New York accent wearing fishnets, leotards, mink and pearls. A bit risqué at fourteen. Backstage, which was basically the school gym, standard 1970s 'light refreshments' were served: orange squash and Rich Tea biscuits. I loved the camaraderie, dressing up and painting our faces, being called to the stage and, of course, the thrill of singing and performing in front of an audience. It's still the same now. Whenever we're on tour there's always a real family feel, although the rider is slightly more elaborate than orange squash and biscuits.

Alongside performing, I loved swimming and belonged to a swimming club that trained twice a week. I even ended up swimming for the county. I also took lessons in lifesaving. We had to jump into the water fully dressed and rescue someone also fully clothed. Part of the test was to remove your outer garments while treading water, tie knots in the end of the trousers or tops, filling them with air so turning them into a float, and then bring your floundering person back to shore. I'm not sure I've ever seen that technique applied in the event of a drowning. I don't think my mother and I had thought it through when we were choosing the clothes to bring for the test. Most children brought light cotton pyjamas; I, however, was given a tight woollen crew neck and a plaid miniskirt that on contact with water became so heavy it made me sink like a stone, my little arms and feet pedalling manically. It was quite traumatising and I wonder why the swimming instructor hadn't pointed it out before I'd got in the pool. Against all odds I got my lifesaving badge and it was proudly sewn to my swimming costume.

Leading up to one of our school's big swimming galas, Keren and I made our first foray into the world of fake tan. We bought a bottle of Coppertone from Boots and headed to my bedroom, opting, for reasons known only to us, to apply it exclusively to our legs. Clearly, we hadn't considered that the stark contrast between tanned lower limbs and the ghostly pallor of our faces and arms would look odd. In any case, after ten minutes, we couldn't see any hint of colour. Determinedly, we applied another layer and slipped our jeans back on. Later that day, the full horror was revealed: streaks of bright orange, covering not only our legs but also our palms. The fact that I was competing in the diving competition as well as the heats, and would be in full view of the entire school, sent me into panic mode. By some miracle the gala ended up being cancelled which meant we were delivered from inevitable humiliation; I was nothing but relieved.

—

KEREN: Sara and I continued to get up to all sorts of mischief, which often saw us landed in detention. On an afternoon when it was lashing with rain, Sara threw a tin of yellow powder paint out of the art room window, accidentally making contact with a bunch of first-year pupils. They were completely coated with it; a yellow stream flowed around the school grounds after them. Firing up Bunsen burners when the chemistry teacher turned his back, and running out first for cross country so we could bomb straight back in after the teacher had gone past, also got us into hot water. Sometimes we played it safe, encouraging others to do our dirty work. On one occasion, we persuaded this girl Julia to lock our teacher in the stationery cupboard, and then didn't let her out until the end of the lesson. Julia also dragged one of the PE teachers around the changing rooms and threw her whistle in the sanitary towel incinerator. This brutal act was payback for the humiliation said teacher had regularly inflicted on us, taking our towels after we'd come out of the showers and leaving us standing in front of everyone, dripping wet and naked, until she decided to return them so we could cover ourselves and scurry back to the benches and hooks where our uniforms were hanging. Some of our teachers really were terrible bullies but, luckily, in our school, girls never got the cane. My brother, on the other hand, received a couple of appalling lashings from the headmaster, once ending up with bleeding welts from his thighs to the base of his back. It was barbaric.

—

SARA: Even when we'd done nothing wrong, we seemed to find ourselves in trouble. Though we were both very sporty and in a wealth of school sports teams, cross country was not something either of us could muster an interest in. For starters, it was generally raining or bitterly cold and miserable. We didn't even have tracksuits, just shorts and flimsy Aertex T-shirts, and we always returned from a run with mottled, red legs, which we christened 'ham legs'. Where's the fun in that? On one occasion, unable to face the dreary trudge of the run, we hid behind some undergrowth on the common. That way, instead of running the full circuit, we could simply lie low for the duration, joining in again right at the end. Unfortunately, some goody-two-shoes grassed and a profanity may have been uttered. It wasn't me who swore at our gym teacher, but I got the blame nonetheless, and this resulted in our banishment from trampoline club which, at the time, was a real blow.

—

KEREN: It's no surprise that when we reached the upper sixth, I was one of the few students who wasn't made a prefect. Neither Sara nor I reacted well at being told what to do, and that's something that hasn't really changed. I was bored by the sixth form anyway; merely biding my time until I left home. I took English and French A-levels, and was talked into Maths by my mum. Pure Mathematics, as it was, was full of formulas and deadly dull, prompting me to ask the teacher at what point in my life it was going to be of any use. When he couldn't answer, I packed up and left the class for good. Unfortunately, the school had already entered me for the exam and insisted I attend. On the day, I sat at the desk and scrawled, 'I AM REFUSING TO TAKE THIS EXAM' across the front of the examination paper. What a rebel!

2

PERMS TO PUNKS

SARA: At sixteen, and on a beautiful sunny afternoon, I found myself lazing under the blossom trees in the school grounds, having offloaded Keats in favour of taking Molly, the English teacher's dog, for a walk. (My teacher, meanwhile, was busy submitting scripts for *The Two Ronnies*.) A-levels approached, and I wasn't sure what direction to take. There was little in the way of school careers advice back then. All I knew was that I wanted to be a writer. But it seemed like an impossible dream. I mean, where did one even go to be a writer, or an actor, or a singer?

I don't know why some people achieve their goals while others fall through the cracks, but I knew I was tenacious and hard-working. I certainly wasn't going to give up on my ambitions. I'd always understood that to achieve anything in life, I had to work hard. Whether it was learning my times tables, running a race or amassing an unfeasible amount of Brownie badges to sew on the arm of my Pixie uniform, I always gave it my best. I lived four doors down from Brown Owl and many's the time that my sister and I would be playing with our dolls on the swing in the garden when we'd hear our names being called. We'd look up to see Brown Owl peering through the honeysuckle in the not-so-distant garden, asking us to come and bag up foil milk bottle tops that were to be sent off and sold, with the resulting money used for guide dogs for the blind. A worthy cause, of course, but not what we wanted to do on a sunny afternoon aged four and seven. Another time when I was trying to gain my House Orderly badge, Brown Owl suggested I clean the bed of her very sweet but quite old dog, on a Saturday just before we went to my grannie's for the afternoon. I think I went for four consecutive weeks; it was absolute torture for a shy seven year old. She and her husband had two teenage children who seemed immensely tall and the four of them would tower over me like giant larch trees, asking questions while I scrubbed away with a cloth stinking of disinfectant and old dog. A very traumatic memory. The things you do for a badge, and a bit of recognition.

As I got older, I realised that life is neither fair nor equal, and that class, gender and race all play a part in the equation. Television in the 1970s and early eighties was often sexist, racist and homophobic and I was lucky to have parents who encouraged me to strive for and achieve the things I wanted in life. I never felt I couldn't do something just because I was a girl.

What you don't have you don't miss, but once you realise it's out there, you want it. I was consumed by music, literature and fashion, and the frustration of not being able to afford something was often hard to bear. I worked Saturday jobs and babysat and kept a meticulous log in my diary, documenting how many weeks it would take before I could afford the pair of Chelsea Girl flares or seven-inch single I coveted. And I can still remember the utter joy of finally being able to make that purchase.

I was only eleven when I started my first job: baby-sitting a small boy whose parents owned a pub, on Saturday afternoons. I enjoyed spending time in the garden with him, collecting big brown fluffy caterpillars. It was talking to adults that terrified me. I was pretty shy and keen to avoid eye contact, so I was always relieved when the five quid in wages was handed over, and I could hotfoot it back to the bus stop. As a teenager, I did a short Saturday-job stint at Littlewoods, and a lengthier one at Jean Machine. The most miserable job, in my quest for financial independence and a pair of platform shoes, entailed sitting in a basement room all day Saturday, peeling onions for pickling. Dustbins full of onions, an awful smell and a paltry wage did not make for a happy working environment. Post that, I lasted one whole day working at a chicken factory with Keren and Lindsey. We had to stick our hands in the trough below their cage where the eggs rolled down. It was too dark to see what you were touching, and some of the eggs didn't have fully formed shells, so were soft and squidgy. The poor battery hens were ultimately sent to market. Local boys would drag them out of their cages, breaking some of their legs on the way, before throwing them into the boxes and onto a waiting lorry. I have no idea where I heard about these grim employment opportunities, but this one was particularly traumatic for me, not to mention the poor birds. After many weeks of hard work, I finally got the platform shoes.

—

KEREN: Saturday jobs meant wages, and wages meant having the funds to buy records and clothes. Before my first job, I had, on the odd occasion, resorted to a bit of light shoplifting. Belts and accessories were easy pickings, as they never seemed to have security tags attached. I'd take them into the changing rooms under an armful of clothes, then just breeze out of the shop wearing them. The odd seven-inch single would also occasionally find itself shoved up inside my Air Force blue tent coat, a voluminous coat with a big pleat at the back which eventually saw its sad demise when Sara and I were sledging down a snowy hill in plastic bread boxes we'd procured from behind the local baker's. I tumbled out, rolling into the road, and the coat was torn to shreds. I only got caught shoplifting once, attempting to slip a white Miners nail varnish up my sleeve, but luckily the woman who collared me just made me put it back on the shelf. I felt sick at the thought of my parents finding out, so this experience was quite the deterrent.

My debut in the workplace was in Woolworths' food department, where I either worked on the till or replenished shelves. I much preferred shelf-replenishment. On the way down from the stockroom in the old lift, I could jam the door, so the lift stopped, giving me enough time to demolish a packet of chocolate biscuits.

I also worked for Marks and Spencer, where the food in the canteen was spectacular. On the downside, I was stationed in the shoe department. I wasn't exactly enamoured with the idea of handling the feet of strangers. The killer blow, however, was the nylon overall I was forced to wear, with nothing showing above or below it. This garment was so horribly unfashionable that I felt compelled to leave the company. Trendy denim outlet, Jean Jeanie, seemed like a much better option, and certainly would have been had it not operated on a commission basis. This was an era of exceptionally tight jeans, and the customers often expected hands-on assistance. I didn't mind some of the time, but highly objected to getting up close and personal with random men in a confined space who needed help getting their zips done up. I'm quite sure that this part of the shopping experience would be deemed inappropriate these days.

—

SARA: In our early teens, we went ice-skating most weekends, where they played the latest chart music as we hurtled around the rink. Keren and I had saved up our Saturday job money and had each bought ourselves a pair of white ice skates, which we decorated with bells and tinsel. We were naturals on the ice. After a while, I bought a pair of ice hockey boots from a jumble sale so I could skate even faster. The two of us perfected a high-speed loop around the rink, in our fashionable jersey smocks with bell-bottoms underneath, with the obligatory abrupt spray stop. We skated to The Fatback Band's 'Do the Bus Stop', Van McCoy's 'The Hustle', Donna Summer's 'Could It Be Magic' and Steve Harley's 'Come Up and See Me (Make Me Smile)'. Fox's 'S-S-S-Single Bed' was a firm favourite, and we eventually covered it on one of our albums.

Keren and I would pool the money we earned to buy records, which we then co-owned. Our first album in this vinyl time-share was *Songs in the Key of Life* by Stevie Wonder. We learned every lyric, backing vocal, harmony, ad-lib, drum beat, chord, cowbell, and even the places where Stevie would take a breath. We were both so passionate about music. After we discovered Roxy Music's *Siren* and *Manifesto* albums, we sought out and bought every record they'd ever made. I loved their album artwork. *For Your Pleasure* was awesome, featuring Amanda Lear in PVC, holding a black panther with a diamond-encrusted collar. Then there was Jerry Hall on *Siren*. She was the first super, supermodel, and I loved her. The *Siren* cover was dramatic, glamorous, arty; in fact, everything I wanted to be. With both Stevie and Roxy, it was the first time I'd heard intelligent lyrics talking about subjects I knew nothing about. Bryan sang in both French and Latin so, naturally, Keren and I did the same. I loved the electro drama of Brian Eno's keys on those early albums and Phil Manzanera's guitar. Subconsciously, we were already learning how to construct songs, and the importance of melody, plus a killer lyric that told a story or evoked a feeling. Watching David Bowie's *Aladdin Sane* concert on TV at Keren's house one evening blew our minds. That was until Keren's dad marched into the living room just as David was snogging a human skull.

He took one look at the screen and switched off the TV, muttering, 'You're not watching that rubbish!'

We were, of course, indignant.

We were still at school when we discovered that Roxy Music were touring their *Manifesto* album and playing near us. We had zero funds and couldn't afford to go, so instead we hung out outside the venue all afternoon. We couldn't believe our eyes when a black limousine drove up and parked at the backstage door. Out stepped Bryan Ferry: black slicked-back hair, black sunglasses and a black Crombie, probably on the way to do his soundcheck.

'Hello ladies,' he said, smiling, at which point we fell to pieces.

'Oh my God! I can't believe we've just met Bryan Ferry dressed like this,' I said.

'Like what?' Keren said.

'Like kids instead of femmes fatales!'

I wasn't a total disaster in my peg trousers and crisp white shirt. In contrast, Keren was wearing kingfisher-blue leggings and a knotted T-shirt that said, 'Shaddap You Face', which was bordering on unforgivable. Something she now hotly disputes.

Later that evening, we waited at the back of the auditorium, peering through the crack in the door at the stage. The lights went down, and the crowd roared. Bryan stepped onto a darkened stage, blowing a cloud of cigarette smoke into a single spotlight, to the strains of 'Love Is the Drug'. It was awesome; the coolest. I also loved his backing singers, especially the Chanter Sisters, with their tight pencil skirts, stilettos and military-style shirts with the glamorous hair and the make-up. Somehow, we eventually managed to bunk in and hid right up in the eaves of the theatre, watching the show.

During that time, Keren and I both experimented with perms, with varying degrees of success. We were trying to attain the Jerry Hall big glam hair and the sexy, shaggy style of Farrah Fawcett in *Charlie's Angels*.

It was around the *Starsky and Hutch*, chunky, long-cardigan period, sometime in the late seventies. I had naturally thick, wavy hair, so once the perming solution took hold, I resembled Hair Bear, from the cartoon *Help! . . . It's The Hair Bear Bunch*. Post-reveal, my mum didn't speak to me for two days, so I tried to tame it by clipping a pink bow on the top to hold it down. However, as a photo-booth picture of Keren and I will attest, it failed spectacularly. Our hair fills the whole photo booth, with two tiny faces peeping out beneath it all. Keren had thinner hair than me, so decided to experiment with Kate Bush-inspired red henna. Her mother had forbidden her to do it, so we locked ourselves in the bathroom while I slapped it on her head. Unfortunately, once it mixed with the perming chemicals, her shaggy hair was left carrot orange. This altered her appearance so dramatically that, a day or so later, her own mother drove past us without recognising her.

It was a time when everything felt like a whirlwind of fun and discovery, always punctuated with music. The soundtrack to my young life began with songs like 'Daydream Believer' by The Monkees, and I remember collecting the cards that came with bubble gum that eventually made up the faces of the group members. I loved Peter, Paul and Mary's 'Leaving on a Jet Plane', which I serenaded my sister with each night, as we shared a bedroom.

My favourite single of the era was 'I'm Still Waiting' by Diana Ross. I loved that song with all my heart: the melody and the lyrics evoked such a sad story. I always wondered where the guy had gone and why. I remember line dancing to Marc Bolan and T. Rex on a PGL-style school trip to the country. We stayed on a derelict army base in army tents that we had to erect ourselves, with about twelve pupils to a tent. Each morning we had to fold the bedding and lay our belongings on top of the bed for inspection. The most orderly tent of the day was awarded a set of deer antlers. Then, at twelve, we were sent out into the wilds on our own to spend the night in a field in a two-man tent. That obviously wouldn't happen now. On the final day of our stay there was a disco in the army barracks and my abiding memory is the magnificent opening guitar riffs of '20th Century Boy' (T. Rex's songs had the most awesome guitar riffs) and me and my friends rushing to the dance floor. I felt just the coolest in my Etam smock which I wore over Primark flares, with a hundred bangles up my arms.

Soul favourites of the time included 'Ms Grace' by The Tymes, 'Back Stabbers' by the O'Jays and the Hues Corporation's 'Rock the Boat'. Then there was the glam of T. Rex, Slade and Sweet, all sequins and feather cuts. I remember seeing Roxy Music sing 'Virginia Plain' on *Top of the Pops* for the first time and, being very young, I wasn't quite sure what to make of Bryan in a feather boa – or was it black sequins? – and blue eye shadow. The sound of the music, however, was so exciting and different to anything else around; I loved its drama. When we were a few years older, Keren and I bought every album they had made, basking in the electronic glory of 'In Every Dream Home a Heartache' in particular. From the avant-garde of Bowie and Roxy Music, to the funk of Parliament and Funkadelic's 'One Nation Under a Groove', Minnie Riperton's 'Lovin' You', Hamilton Bohannon and Barry White to punks, Sex Pistols, Clash and Blondie, and not forgetting Donna Summer's 'Love to Love You Baby', and so many more, Keren and I were immersed in an unashamed mixture of disco, funk, glam, arty rock and punk.

Like most kids in the 1970s, our main window into the world of music was *Top of the Pops*, every Thursday night. As much as I loved watching it, though, it always seemed to be awash with smooth American male vocalists or macho rock bands.

Positive female role models are so important for girls growing up. Seeing other women achieve great things is inspiring and helps you to envision that potential in yourself. But they were few and far between when I was young. I had confidence in my abilities: I just had no idea how to channel or focus them. As a child, the TV and entertainment landscape was endless *Match of the Day*, snooker, darts, motor racing, John Wayne movies, and strutting male rock stars. So, when Blondie burst onto the scene, fronted by the incredible Debbie Harry, I was truly blown away. She was so cool and, while there was no denying her raw, pouting beauty was a significant selling point, she was so much more – she had an edge.

Blondie's tracks were brilliant melodic pop, but they'd been around in New York for years, coming up through the ranks of punk and New Wave before they eventually cracked it. As I watched Debbie perform 'Picture This' – a vision in a yellow pencil dress with bleached white hair swooping over one eye and dyed black at the back – I thought she looked like a goddess. I imagined how glamorous and cool New York must be, never dreaming that one day I would be celebrating my own number one record there.

Women had been so sidelined that even seeing Debbie Harry do her thing on *Top of the Pops* didn't make me think, 'Oh, right! I can do that!' That level of achievement seemed so very far out of reach. Still, it did start to feel like there were more and more women putting their heads above the pop parapet. Patti Smith had a profound effect on me, not just for her music but for introducing me to the whole subculture of New York. I discovered authors like William Burroughs, Gore Vidal and Truman Capote, and artists and photographers like Robert Mapplethorpe. I loved Poly Styrene from X-Ray Spex, whose album, *Germfree Adolescents*, I played over and over in my bedroom with my little sister. Siouxsie Sioux, Gaye Advert, and Viv Albertine with her band The Slits all made me feel there was a place for women in music. They opened my eyes to a new and exciting world and I had an unquenchable thirst for it.

—

KEREN: We were about fifteen when we graduated from school discos to real clubs and proper gigs. Despite looking ridiculously young, nobody ever asked us for ID. Imagine a fifteen-year-old kid being able to wander into a pub or club and order drinks these days; it just wouldn't happen. Back then, however, there were plenty of places we could get into with nobody batting an eyelid. Platform shoes and stilettos helped at least make us taller, and we assumed that carrying a handbag would also add to a mature, sophisticated look. On my fifteenth birthday, Sara bought me the twelve-inch single of T-Connection's 'Do What You Wanna Do', which was the best present I'd ever had. That night, I donned my black satin boob-tube and gold Lurex skinny trousers, and we headed out to a club.

We got in, which was the first hurdle, and then ordered a couple of vodka and limes at the bar. We hadn't been sure what to ask for, but that was Sara's dad's tipple of choice, I think, so it seemed a viable option. It was either that or my mother's revolting favourite, Cinzano and lemonade, or, as she pronounced it, Sinzano.

We danced the night away, and I snogged someone called Vince the baker. At the end of the night, we headed to the taxi rank, which seemed the sensible thing to do at 2 a.m. Just as we were getting chatted up by some attractive older men, my dad turned up in our white Morris Marina, completely blowing our cool. He'd been cruising around looking for us, and I was furious. Dad never changed in that respect. In fact, when I was fifty, I returned to my parents' house after an evening out, around midnight, only to find him patiently waiting for me at the window. My friend's son was dropping me off, and couldn't believe it.

'Dad, I'm fifty!' I said.

'I know but I couldn't relax until I knew you were home safely.'

Ridiculous, but very sweet. And I'd do the same with my son, Tom. After all, your kids are always your kids, no matter how old they are.

My younger brother Matt and his friends had a three-piece band who played songs by The Jam, like 'In the City' and 'This Is the Modern World'. I generously allowed rehearsals to take place in my bedroom as Matt only had a box room, and we frequently bunked off school to hang out and listen to music – 'No More Heroes' and 'Peaches' by The Stranglers, as well as The Damned and Sham 69; we loved a bit of Elvis Costello too. I got caught a couple of times, as Auntie Meg was head of music, and when my absence was noted, she'd call Mum and I'd get a real tongue lashing. After I passed my driving test at seventeen, I drove my brother and his mates to a real Jam gig in the Morris Marina. I'm not sure how I managed to persuade Dad to let me borrow it, given the first time I took it out, with Sara, I'd managed to crash it three times: once in a car park, once into some railings on a flyover, and then into the gate post as I arrived home.

Sara and I spent a lot of time in London. The train journey took just over an hour from Bristol, so we'd visit the capital whenever we could. In our early teens it was day trips for shopping, but by sixth form we occasionally told our parents that we were each staying at the other's house. We'd catch the train earlier in the day, giving us plenty of time to explore, and sometimes go to gigs in the early evening. Of course, we had no mobile phones, and nobody knew where the hell we were, so it was an incredibly stupid thing to do.

—

SARA: We'd exchange the vouchers we'd collected from the back of cornflake boxes for free train tickets and from around the age of fourteen, we spent many a Saturday 'up west' at Topshop in Oxford Circus. We could never afford anything but it was just so exciting being surrounded by fashion and imagining what our dream wardrobes would look like.

On one particular Saturday we ventured to the King's Road and were sitting on the steps of Chelsea Town Hall. Resplendent in our drainpipe jeans, mohair striped jumpers and plastic sandals, we watched the punks go by. After a while, an 'old' guy sat down beside us and started a conversation. It was Keith Richards from the Rolling Stones! Although there was an unwritten rule that punks weren't supposed to like old rockers, he was so cool, funny and totally relaxed. He seemed really interested in our clothes and the music we liked and so we relaxed and chatted back.

Later, when a policeman appeared, having been tipped off by a member of the public that Keren was sniffing glue – because apparently that's what some punks did – Keith helped us sort the situation out and Keren opened her crumpled Boots bag to reveal not glue but a disposable camera and accompanying flash Magicube. Years later, while we were on a promo trip to Australia, a journalist told us he'd recently interviewed Mr Richards. Apparently when he'd asked Keith what was happening in London right now, he'd replied, 'Those little girls who are swimming with fish on their album cover.' Bananarama, *Deep Sea Skiving*!

The King's Road was a punk's paradise; a catwalk for strutting up and down. Keren and I loved soaking up the atmosphere. We were too young and nervous to enter Malcolm McLaren and Vivienne Westwood's shop, SEX, at World's End. Instead, we stared in awe from the safety of a vintage clothes store called 20th Century Box, which was on the opposite side of the street. Sometimes, we'd head to Kensington Market, which is where we'd eventually meet the London DJ, Fat Tony, with whom we instantly hit it off. How could you not love someone who jokingly told you he was on a diet while he had a big Mac stuffed in his overcoat pocket. On a few occasions, we ventured into another major punk haunt, Beaufort Market. Everybody seemed so intimidatingly cool with their dyed spiky hair and SEX bondage tops, festooned with studs and chains; they looked completely different. We tended to shuffle around without a penny in our pocket, desperate to look like we belonged there but terrified that someone would speak to us.

—

KEREN: As we didn't have the money for fashionable punk gear, like bondage trousers, we started what would be a long tradition of DIY as far as outfits went. Drainpipes and my favourite pointy boots with metal tips, teamed with one of my uncle's old police shirts with a few strategically placed rips, were the order of the day. I sometimes accessorised with my dad's paratrooper tie slung loosely around my neck. I'd have preferred a skinny black one, but Dad's tie rail was full of gigantic, garish kippers. I pierced my own ears three times with a safety pin which I left in until they went septic, and the safety pins had to be replaced with gold sleepers and studs.

—

SARA: We were dying to be part of the punk tribe but joining was hindered somewhat by the fact that we were not old enough to get into clubs. Back home we did, however, manage to get in to some punk gigs. They were often in small pubs or local halls and clubs, and were advertised in the music papers or on posters in town. We saw The Police and Generation X, whose lead singer Billy Idol winked at us from the stage, sending our hearts racing. On that occasion, we'd changed out of our school uniforms and stuffed them into carrier bags. I wore black, satin 'Fruit Fly' drainpipes, a ripped Clash T-shirt and plastic sandals, which now seem like a hideous choice of shoe. Later that year we saw Sham 69, Ian Dury and the Blockheads, Siouxsie and the Banshees, The Damned, The Ramones and The Clash, who were supported by one of my favourite bands, The Slits. Viv Albertine had a guitar around her neck: she was anarchic, rebelling against every female stereotype. I really related to her and loved her style: her messy blond hair, the tutu and DMs. It was a look I became very fond of several years later.

It was while we were at a Ramones gig that we both got carried away, literally feet off the ground, in a frenzied mosh pit of pogoing. After a few minutes of this crushed, hot and sweaty ritual, and with the air raining phlegm from all the spitting, we looked at each other as if to say, *what the hell are we doing this for?* In the end, we fought our way to the side of the ballroom and enjoyed the band from there.

—

KEREN: Though we loved the vibe and raw excitement of those nights, Sara and I realised pretty early on that pogoing and getting covered in gob wasn't for us.

As well as making our own clothes and customising

outfits from our parents' wardrobes, we also borrowed from the trendiest shop in town, with the owner's blessing, taking stuff back once we'd had our night out. It was a small boutique in an underpass, full of clothes that were more like those we'd seen in Beaufort Market on the King's Road than in the shops on the local high street. I actually bought two of my all-time favourite items from there: a dark blue/green mohair cardigan that I kept for years, and some black 'Strawberry Studio' drainpipe jeans with zip pockets and ankles. The shop's owner was a dapper guy who dressed in a fifties style, with vintage leather jackets, drainpipes and winklepickers. He also had a convertible Cadillac, the likes of which we'd only seen on our favourite American cop shows, like *Starsky and Hutch* and *Kojak*, and we were always excited to be taken for the odd spin around town in it.

To get to this shopping paradise, we'd have to persuade two boys we knew to take us on the back of their motorbikes a couple of times a week after school. However, we didn't consider them to be all that cool – at least not as cool as us – so insisted that they wore their full-face helmets for the journey there and back. They certainly weren't cool enough to accompany us inside the shop, where we'd enjoy hanging out with the regulars. The deal was that they simply dropped us and came back to collect us at a pre-arranged time.

—

SARA: I've always enjoyed the creative buzz from putting outfits together with bits and pieces from second-hand stores. I mixed my mum's 1960s clothes with some less expensive items from the high street, picking up fabric from the market, wrapping swathes of my mum's necklaces around my neck and wearing her long black evening gloves. By this time, we were veering between punk gigs, discos and funk clubs.

—

KEREN: The funk club we loved was small but because we were suitably attired, and possibly because the owner of our favourite shop had put in a word, we always got in. Batwing tops, boob tubes, even the odd slinky pencil skirt worked for me, but I also coveted the fabulous leopard-print dress that Sara wore. We danced the night away to songs like 'Stuff Like That' by Quincy Jones or Hamilton Bohannon's 'Let's Start The Dance'. The club's clientele was always very glamorously dressed, and it felt more like an exclusive members' club than the bigger, generic discos we'd been to.

—

SARA: For the school disco in 1979, I attempted to emulate Bianca Jagger's Studio 54 look. I borrowed my dad's black suit jacket, white shirt and black tie, which I wore with black satin cigarette pants and stilettos, and I have a sneaking suspicion I was rocking a loose perm. I thought I looked fabulous, dancing to Earth, Wind & Fire's 'Boogie Wonderland'. As far as I was concerned, I'd arrived that night!

3

WEST END GIRLS

KEREN: On a glorious summer's day in 1980, I left home, aged eighteen. I was nervous, to say the least, heading for my very first job, with absolutely no idea what was in store for me. My suitcase was minuscule. In fact, these days I'd barely consider it a weekend bag. There certainly weren't enough clothes inside it to fill the single wardrobe and chest of drawers provided in the shared room at the YWCA Great Russell Street, which was my destination.

I'd applied to join the BBC as soon as I'd finished my A-levels. At school, the careers officer had suggested I consider becoming a bilingual secretary or air hostess, due to an apparent talent for languages, which, sadly, I have let slide along with the piano skills. I hadn't a clue what I wanted to do, except that, whatever it was, it had to be in London, and a job in radio or perhaps even TV appealed. Arriving for my interview I was told that I was to head over to the pensions department for a further interview. Pensions? That didn't sound like me at all. I was appalled and cursed my grade A Maths O-level. Still, I'd been assured that once I had my foot in the door, BBC employees always had the first pick of any upcoming vacancies, so that was the notion to which I clung.

All I needed was a chance to shine, surely. My mother had encouraged me to wear the smart royal-blue silk dress she'd run up on her trusty Singer. I teamed it with a pair of fetching new heels from Dolcis and wore my freshly dyed, blue/black hair smoothed down, so it didn't look too scary. It wasn't at all my usual style but obviously worked because I got the job. Not only that, but the boss apparently announced the arrival of 'a cracker' joining the workforce. I'm not sure how he felt about my subsequent parade of outfits. Needless to say, I didn't ever look anything like I had at my interview again.

At the YWCA hostel, situated in Helen Graham House in Holborn, I was assigned a single bed in a huge room overlooking the British Museum. The room was to be shared with two other girls, a Turkish girl who didn't speak much English, and a nice girl called Helen from East Anglia. As you might imagine, there wasn't much glamour to be had at the YWCA. Each floor had a warden on patrol, like a prison, and a kitchen equipped with a kettle and little else. There were a couple of shared bathrooms, housing huge iron baths, which were generally adorned with filthy water-rings, and a découpage of hair and soap scum. And while hygiene might not have been high on the list of priorities, there were plenty of other rules and regulations to adhere to. The main door was locked promptly at 10 p.m. – after that, you had to ring the bell, and the lovely old porter would shuffle to the door and let you in. No boys were allowed further than the reception area, not that I minded, being single.

With the kitchen not being up to much, my diet was dreadful, with cooking methods amounting to heating tins of baked beans in the kettle, and then eating them with Smash – instant mash. That said, a breakfast of sorts was provided in the basement of the building, consisting of a cup of tea and a wizened brown roll, served with individually wrapped butter pats and jam. I generally skipped this feast and went instead to the small BBC cafeteria area provided in my office building at 2 Cavendish Square. When I eventually arrived at my desk, clutching doughnuts and crisps, I'd settle down to a day of doing as little work as I thought I could get away with.

That said, I liked the office I was working in, and particularly my section. My direct superior was a lovely man called Nicos Christodoulou; he was very sweet and softly spoken. Years later, when I had my son, Tom, I remembered his sage advice about not letting your child sleep in the bed. 'You'll never get them out again, Keren,' he said.

We laughed a lot and, down the line, when I started clubbing till all hours, Nicos was a saint. On hungover mornings, I'd sometimes go into the small computer room for a nap, and Nicos would knock on the door to alert me if the boss was around. For a while, I was on flexi-time, but the powers that be eventually put a stop to that. I owed them so many hours I'd have had to work there for decades to make them up.

There was a lovely young punky boy who worked in the neighbouring office called David Caines, who sometimes came clubbing with Sara and me. He was a massive Joy Division fan and ran into my office, grief-stricken, when Ian Curtis died. Eventually he too escaped the BBC finance department to go to Chelsea College of Arts. We remained friends long after we'd both left the BBC, and the first painting I ever bought was a massive canvas of his work. I'm glad to say that he is still an artist to this day.

If nothing else, my time at the BBC let me experience my one and only office Christmas party. All normal office behaviour went straight out of the window and the big surprise came when a shy colleague grabbed me for a snog under the mistletoe. It was surprisingly raucous, with everybody bringing their own booze. But that was about as exciting as it got in the pensions department of the BBC and, as pleasant as my office was, I was reasonably sure I wasn't cut out for the routine of nine to five.

—

SARA: I'm a North London girl, I've lived here since my teens. Apart from a couple of years in WC1 and WC2, North London has always been my home: Kentish Town, Archway, Highgate, Hampstead, and

St John's Wood. London is a magnet for creative spirits and alive with the wonderful, diverse culture.

And I love the parks. I've visited Hampstead Heath for as long as I can remember with friends, family, kids and dogs; it re-energises me. It's rambling and hilly, with lakes and ponds, and ancient woodlands. It has the most spectacular views over the city and when I was pregnant I would sit at the top of Parliament Hill happily contemplating the future, watching people fishing around the glistening lake and children flying kites.

With the kids I've climbed trees, built snowmen, sledged down hills and swam in the ponds. I love sitting in the garden at Kenwood House with a coffee, people watching or watching the lakeside concerts, held there in summer.

It's a world away from the London of the early eighties, where clutching my grey, plastic overnight case with my monkey boots tied to the handle I boarded a bus, and sat on the top deck, hoping it would drop me somewhere vaguely near the YWCA. The lights of the city twinkled and I breathed in the cool air with a feeling of excitement. This was my first taste of independence.

I arrived at the hostel and climbed the wide, stone steps of the grand-looking building, pushed the door open and found myself in the cavernous reception area. The grandeur of the exterior had in no way continued inside. It all felt very dreary, yellowing paint running through echoing corridors. At the desk, an elderly porter took me to a room to deposit my first week's rent, which was £14.50, and then showed me to my room.

I was about to start a journalism course at the London College of Fashion, part of the University of the Arts near Oxford Circus, which I'd seen advertised in the back pages of *Vogue*. At fourteen I had sent a script proposal to Barry Norman's film review show on the BBC. They were running a competition for young scriptwriters and film hopefuls. It came back with a letter saying 'very commendable'; I was thrilled that they had at least responded. I was always entering writing competitions in magazines and winning book vouchers and concert tickets. Finally, on a school trip, I'd attended a lecture by the poet Ted Hughes at Bristol University and I was convinced I wanted to be a writer. The writing world seemed to be male-dominated but I'd been discovering some incredible female writers like Stevie Smith, Edith Sitwell, Sylvia Plath, Simone de Beauvoir, Doris Lessing and Virginia Woolf, among others, and this felt like my calling.

Though my A-levels were good, I hadn't been confident of getting a place. According to the principal who interviewed me for the course at seventeen, there were only sixty places, which didn't sound like a lot, given the number of applicants. At the end of the interview he asked me to walk up and down in his office as if it were a catwalk and he told me if I didn't get a place on the journalism course, I should enrol on the modelling course that was on offer. I was flattered, naïvely, positive that the cream, knee-length boots I'd borrowed from a school friend, and the Studio 54-style dress from Chelsea Girl, had made some sort of impact. My look *du jour* was topped off with a Farrah Fawcett-Majors-style blow wave. I'd recently seen a photograph of Jerry with her gorgeous *Siren* hair, papped with Bryan Ferry as they left a neon-drenched nightclub and I remember thinking, *where is that glamorous life? I want it!*

My room was on a different floor to Keren's. I was to be sharing with a girl from Newcastle, who was training to be a beauty therapist, and a design student from Manchester. The room looked very uninviting: against each wall stood three white metal beds, which I was convinced came from an asylum, topped with scratchy beige blankets. The ceilings were high, the walls magnolia, and there was lino on the floors. There was nothing vaguely cosy or homely about it and putting anything up on the walls was forbidden. Still, rebel that I was, I eventually plastered it with pictures of Marlon Brando from *On the Waterfront*, Patti Smith, Viv Albertine and Bob Marley. Anything to get rid of the institutionalised feel of the place. That first night at the hostel, sleeping in a room with two strangers while my best friend was on another floor, felt weird and a little lonely. I pushed my suitcase under the bed, wrapped my mum's cherry-red cardigan around me for comfort, and climbed into bed.

In the morning, I found myself in the enormous old hall where an *Oliver Twist*-style dining experience awaited us, with old cream plates stacked high and giant urns of coffee laid out on trestle tables. It wouldn't be long before I was stocking up on the dry bread rolls that they served each morning, just to keep me going. I was on a student grant, so most of the time it was a toss-up between shopping for clothes or eating. As you might imagine, shopping often won the day.

There were, I think, only two bathtubs for the entire floor at the YWCA, and each bathroom was no bigger than the heavy pre-war bath it housed. Still, once it was my turn to bathe, sinking into the big, deep tub after a hard day's night felt like pure luxury. Even the intermittent banging on the bathroom door, urging me to hurry up, couldn't spoil the moment. Once out of the bath, it was a dash back to the room, which was freezing in the winter, but equipped with a two-bar heater, high on the wall, operated by a pull-cord. The trouble was, the meter had to be fed 50p before it worked and, as we couldn't afford that most of the time, we usually froze. Still, we were happy with our newfound independence. We were smack bang in the middle of the West End and there seemed to be so much promise out there, so many possibilities. This was going to be the start of a great adventure for Keren and me.

On the day I arrived at the London College of Fashion for induction, the hall was packed with hundreds of students from all the different courses. There were some interesting sights to behold: a girl with a shaved head and bright BIBA-pink eye make-up, would-be designers with weird, eccentric clothes, and the uni grads who, at twenty-three, seemed so much more grown up and confident than me. I stood on my own in the crowd in my electric kingfisher-blue Topshop trousers, my old, familiar Clash T-shirt, monkey boots and crimped blond hair. I felt very young and slightly nervous. I thought I was the only eighteen-year-old school leaver on the course until I found Lindsey from North London. The two of us giggled excitedly together and became instant friends.

As people started to organise themselves into their respective course groups, I spotted someone across the room. I thought she had quite a similar look to me: baggy Levi's, a baggy red jumper, monkey boots and black crimped hair. It was Siobhan Fahey. I don't think we spoke then, but at lunchtime, when I met up with Keren, I told her I'd spotted a girl who I knew would be my friend.

Siobhan was twenty-one and living with her boy-friend, Jim, which seemed immensely grown up to me. She'd decided to go back to college after a stint working at Decca Records I think. Of course, I couldn't have imagined, that day, what an important part of my life she'd end up being, or the bond we'd eventually form. Even though we've had our ups and downs over the years, she's part of my history and always will be.

Despite our similar aesthetic, Siobhan's upbringing had been very different from Keren's and mine. Her father was in the British army so she'd spent most of her early childhood moving from one army base to another.

Once we'd started getting to know one another,

Siobhan introduced me to her friend, Mel. The three of us would go for lunch at Ponti's, an Italian restaurant opposite the college. As Siobhan was living with Jim and we had different sets of friends, she and I didn't really hang out much outside college at first but we sat together in lectures most days. Usually at the back of the class with our little gang of friends, Lindsey, Sandra and Jane, who had uber-fashionable, Vidal Sassoon-styled, geometric black and white hair.

One of the many things I remember about Siobhan from our time at college were hair disasters. On one occasion, I accidentally set her fringe on fire with a match; on another, her hair snapped off when a beauty course student gave her some highlights for free, using the old-fashioned rubber swim cap with little holes for the hair to be pulled through.

As part of the course, we had to do a lot of vox pops. Rather than approaching strangers around Oxford Circus to ask their opinions, we quite often just made them up over a coffee in Ponti's. We'd then have to return to college to give a speech on our findings in front of the class, which Siobhan and I both found excruciating. There was an organised trip to Paris for Fashion Week but I couldn't afford it as I was on a student grant.

We shared a love of music: Patti Smith, Talking Heads, Joy Division, Soft Cell and various electronic music. Plus a mental, mischievous sense of humour that later kept us going through many a long promo tour. This same sense of humour once meant we were deported to a caravan in the car park on the German equivalent of

Banished to the car park, German TV.

Top of the Pops after too much messing around backstage; we had crashed into the set while David Christie was performing 'Saddle Up'.

—

KEREN: When my roommate left and Sara was able to move into my room, it felt like life really had begun. Relishing our newfound freedom, we played our David Bowie records – notably *Heroes* and the *Low* album – loud. Sara would balance her typewriter on the end of the bed and work on assignments. We hung our wet washing from the wall ledges. We lived on Pot Noodles, bread and whatever fitted in the kettle. For a short while, we still had a third wheel in the form of another roommate, but she would eventually move out, unable to cope with our late hours and general wildness.

In the grim TV lounge – and I use the term 'lounge' in its very loosest terms – we met Ziggy and Debbie, who were also residents of the YWCA. It probably won't come as a surprise to hear that Ziggy, real name Mandy, dressed like David Bowie in his Ziggy Stardust phase, wearing outfits that included a satin high-necked mini dress and boots. Ziggy was keen to introduce us to London nightlife and was the first person to take us to The Blitz club, which was when we started clubbing with a vengeance.

The Blitz was so far removed from any experience we'd ever had before. Everyone was dressed up, and each person's look was a new thrill. In fact, if you didn't look like you'd made an effort to look fabulous, you wouldn't be allowed through the door. The club's host and door-whore extraordinaire, Steve Strange, saw to that, famously turning away Mick Jagger. Of course, we were there the night it happened!

Inside the dark recesses of the club, which was held in a wine bar in Great Queen Street, boys wore make-up and some wore what most people would consider women's clothes, which I found fascinating. Up until then, my only experience of gender-bending, as it was then known, was Dick Emery and Danny La Rue prancing around on Christmas TV specials. These boys – the Blitz Kids, as they came to be known – re-wrote the narrative. Stylish peacocks, who preened and posed with cigarette holders and cocktails, they certainly weren't there to be laughed at, although I must admit to the odd snigger.

The girls were equally fabulous, blurring lines and redesigning femininity, wearing white faces, cupid-bow lips, 1940s hairstyles and lashes that could sweep the floor. Smiles, overall, were a no-no, because it cracked the facade of poised perfection. While I loved the place, I sometimes found all the posing and posturing faintly ridiculous. As much as Sara and I were particular about our appearance, the main aim was, as it still is, to have as much fun as we possibly could. Club DJ Rusty Egan played 'The Model' by Kraftwerk, 'Heroes' by David Bowie, 'Electricity' by OMD and early Human League, while people danced in pairs. Sara and I were there so often, we quickly began to meet new people, possibly fuelled by alcohol, which was something else we were quite inexperienced with.

—

SARA: The Blitz had already been up and running for a while, so we were on the tail end of it, having only just left school. Our style was more the remnants of our punk phase fused with stuff from vintage markets like Portobello and Camden; we weren't huge fans of the frilly blouses and headbands favoured by the New Romantics. That said, the lengths people went to when dressing up for a night at The Blitz meant that many of the outfits were amazing sights to behold. On our first evening, I looked around the room, drinking it all in, mesmerised by all the 'beautiful' people and loving the fantastic new electronic sound. I wasn't quite as fond of what seemed to be the customary dance, which involved holding hands and lifting one knee at a time. Keren and I gave that a wide berth.

We ended up making many friends from the crowd at The Blitz including Mark Moore, who went on to form S'Express, and together we'd travel all over London to different house parties and clubs.

One night, Keren, Ziggy, Debbie and I went to the Scala, a big club in King's Cross, to see a new band, who were all Blitz Kids. Spandau Ballet arrived on stage, swathed in tweed trousers and kilts, looking very serious. We weren't sure what to make of the clothes but the music and the crowd were exciting. *London Weekend Live* were filming there that night and I ended up being part of the opening titles of the show each week, all big hair and nonchalant attitude.

Aside from The Blitz, we also briefly frequented a club on Oxford Street called Studio 21, which was where we first met future Bananarama member, Jacquie O'Sullivan. I also met an androgynous lesbian, who was dressed as David Bowie circa the *Low* album, as well as a chart-topping male pop star, who I was surprised to see pairing his customary smart suit with high heels and chandelier earrings. Then there was the guy who, around midnight, would swoop down the staircase like the Wicked Witch of the West, resplendent in black, with a cape billowing behind him and cerise eye make-up. This turned out to be Boy George, and he was usually with his friend, Jeremy Healey, who had a snake painted around his neck. Jeremy went on to form the band Haysi Fantayzee before becoming a world-renowned DJ. It was all very dramatic and exciting. Bizarrely, but brilliantly, the club handed out food vouchers at the door. Keren and I would eagerly await the nightly serving-up of burger and chips. As ever, our lack of funds meant that our clubbing outfits always involved some creative customising of old clothes from charity shops. I remember adding studs to my grannie's old suede snow boots, and they looked fabulous, and much more original than a pair I might have bought in a shop.

—

KEREN: Post clubbing, we'd often go to the twenty-four-hour canteen at Broadcasting House for a fry-up, until I was reprimanded and asked not to. Still, my BBC pass came in very handy. Each week, when *Top of the Pops* was being recorded, we'd go to the BBC club bar in Shepherd's Bush and check out which pop stars were hanging around. We'd then tell the security guards we were part of their entourage, so we could get in and infiltrate the studio audience. We made it onto quite a few shows before someone twigged, at which point we weren't allowed near the place – until we were actually performing on the show. Looking back, I think we were far more energetic as audience members than we were as performers in those early days.

Sara spent hours teasing her hair into magnificent massiveness, with a combination of hair crimpers and backcombing. She caused quite a stir as we walked from

Great Russell Street to Oxford Street. My hair was short and blue-black until I unwisely decided I wanted peroxide white. I went to the hair and beauty students at the London College of Fashion where, after their third attempt, I had what looked like pale yellow cotton wool on top of a red-raw scalp. The perils of peroxide, however, were not particular to me. One evening, Sara was lying on the floor of our room, and I accidentally walked over her hair. When she sat up, a sizeable chunk of it remained on the lino.

The wellbeing of our hair, however, wasn't high up on our list of priorities; it was the look and the image that was all-important. We were good at dressing up and looking fabulous and there was always something to dress up for. Constant party invitations often saw us trekking to distant, far-flung corners of London that were utterly alien to us. I'd met a boy who lived in Cricklewood and one evening he took me to meet eccentric club entrepreneur Philip Sallon. I was hugely shocked that, although Philip lived at home with his parents, he was quite comfortable showing off his freshly-dyed electric-blue pubic hair.

—

SARA: Being West End girls meant that if the party was in south London, we'd occasionally end up crashing on someone's living room floor. We'd wake up the next morning under a pile of coats, dust ourselves down, and head off to college or work in the same clothes.

We fast got used to people staring at us on public

transport because of the way we looked and, as time went on, we relished the fact that our shock value was so high. In the BBC lift with Keren one day, comedian Peter Cook stared at me in the mirror, pulling faces. I was wearing my brand new, 'New Wave' pink and black drainpipes from Topshop, my mum's sixties winkle-picker shoes, and freshly crimped hair piled up in a messy side ponytail. He seemed highly amused.

Our partying experiences became even more exciting when we met Youth, from the band Killing Joke. He lived in a squat in Notting Hill with the rest of his bandmates, and his best mate, Alex Paterson, who later co-founded The Orb. Keren and I spent quite a bit of time hanging out at their place. We frequented various parties in Notting Hill and Ladbroke Grove with him, where he introduced us to a cast of weird and wonderful characters. We were a couple of teenagers, keenly exploring a vibrant, alien landscape, and taking it all in our stride. We couldn't have imagined then we'd end up working with Youth ten years later, on our *Pop Life* album.

Looking back there's one mid-Sunday morning, after a late Saturday night, that seems like the catalyst for so much that happened afterwards.

Male visitors to the YWCA were announced over the tannoy, which boomed down the corridors.

'Sara Dallin, Keren Woodward, there is a Paul Cook for you in reception.'

'Paul Cook from the Sex Pistols?' we both screeched in disbelief.

Bolting out of bed, we grabbed our clothes as fast as

we could, hoping he'd wait for us, then ran full-pelt down the long corridor, slowing up as we got to the stairs so as not to appear *très* uncool. We'd met Paul briefly the night before, at Studio 21, and one of us must have told him where we lived. Now, here he was on a Sunday morning, offering to take us for a drive – yes, a drive – in his BMW convertible. Not only that, but he wanted to take us for lunch in Soho.

This was mind-blowing. Here we were, jumping into a BMW with one of our punk heroes. At the time, it was the most exciting thing that could ever happen.

4

I DON'T KNOW WHERE THOSE TWO CAME FROM BUT SUDDENLY THEY WERE EVERYWHERE . . .

SARA: In the ensuing months, Paul became like a big brother to us, always making sure we were OK, and taking us to cool places where we'd meet people whose posters had been on our walls when we were kids, like Joe Strummer and Paul Simenon from The Clash. If we weren't at some fabulous house party in Mayfair, we'd be hanging out at his flat in Bell Street, Lisson Grove, with his friend Nils Stevenson and Steve Severin from Siouxsie and the Banshees.

—

KEREN: One night, Paul took us for a meal at a friend's flat in Notting Hill. Known as the wizard, he was a guy we'd seen around quite a bit. He had tattoos all over his face. We sat cross-legged on the floor around a chalked zodiac chart and were served stew. I'm not sure precisely what was in it, but from the way I felt afterwards, I'm guessing magic mushrooms were a key ingredient. I was too naïve to know what I was doing, but certainly too shy to decline (I think Sara pretended to eat it). After we'd spent a bit of time sweating and giggling nervously from either side of the circle, Sara glared and I knew exactly what she was saying, 'Let's get out of here, away from these old hippies!' Acting as cool as we could, under the circumstances, we extricated ourselves from the zodiac circle and crept out. We didn't want to appear rude, but I'm sure they were too stoned to even notice we'd gone.

God knows what time we got back home again. The poor old porter at the hostel must have been sick to death of the two of us, making him shuffle up and down to the door to let us in at all hours of the night. So much so, that eventually we were called into the YWCA office for a talking-to. We weren't all that bothered. By that point, we'd already been warned that the place was being closed for refurbishment. We were basically being thrown out anyway.

—

SARA: Just as Keren and I were about to become homeless, Paul Cook came to the rescue. He and ex-Sex Pistols guitarist, Steve Jones, still owned a rehearsal room in Denmark Street, also known as Tin Pan Alley, just off Charing Cross Road, with their former-manager Malcolm McLaren's office above it. Paul suggested that we move in and, even better, we could live there rent-free.

Glamorous it was not. We entered our new home through a long, dark corridor between a Greek bookshop and a small club also called Tin Pan Alley, which led into a courtyard. And when I say courtyard, I mean a scruffy, dirty, small square with a filthy outside toilet on one side. On the opposite side of the square was a makeshift shack, which looked like something Robinson Crusoe might have built. There was a heavy wooden sound-proofed door that led to a steep flight of narrow, felt-covered stairs up to a small office. The smell of damp hit us immediately; something we were already accustomed to from washing our clothes in the sink at the hostel, then hanging them up to drip dry from the walls.

As we reached the top of the stairs, we were confronted by murals of Sid and Nancy, Malcolm McLaren, Steve Jones with a pot belly, and various slogans, all painted, we were told, by John Lydon. The room contained two enormous polystyrene 'O's, one from 'ROCK', one from 'ROLL', props left over from the film *The Great Rock 'n' Roll Swindle*. There was also a giant Bambi, from the video for the song 'Who Killed Bambi?' which I ended up using as my headboard, and a neon sign that said 'New Oldies Club'. Other luxuries included a sink with cold running water and a cupboard full of Sex Pistols stationery, plus a pair of Sid Vicious's old bondage trousers.

We set about furnishing the place. First, we 'borrowed' two mattresses from the hostel, wheeling them along Great Russell Street on the night porter's tea trolley. It

Our names still on the wall after all these years, Denmark Street.

was our lucky day, though, as a guy in a Rolls-Royce pulled up and offered to lend us a hand, doubling our mattresses over and stuffing them in the back of his car. We used one of the letter Os as a coffee table and piled all our clothes under a bench table near the windows. Once settled, we added our names to Lydon's mural, which remains there to this day – now a protected heritage site.

The best thing about our hovel was its location. We could walk straight into Soho, which made it perfect for clubbing. Below the office was the room where the Sex Pistols had once rehearsed and was now used by Paul and Steve's new band, The Professionals. It must have been weird for Paul and Steve, having these two teenage urchins living above their rehearsal room. Whenever they arrived to rehearse, we'd rush down to join them, and they seemed more than happy to set up the mics for us to sing backing vocals. Steve taught me to play The Velvet Underground's 'White Light/White Heat' on the bass and Paul, on occasion, tried patiently to teach our friend Mel the drums. She wasn't too bad but wore an incredibly intense look on her face while getting faster and faster until she was totally out of time with everyone else and we'd all crack up laughing. I can still hear Paul's distinctive laugh. There was nothing Keren and I loved more than coming in from a club late at night, then heading to the rehearsal room and plugging in the guitars for a spot of heavy-duty jamming.

A few years later, Paul remarked to someone, 'I don't know where those two came from, but suddenly they were everywhere.' Suffice to say I think he adored us as we adored him. We stayed great friends, with Paul ending up playing on tracks from our 1991 album, *Pop Life*. He also played on several European TV shows with us in the nineties. One of those shows was particularly memorable because the act before us was spinning plates. When it all went horribly wrong, with the plates crashing to the floor, all we could hear was Paul, with that laugh again, as we all collapsed in hysterics in the wings.

The Professionals began recording an album at Richard Branson's residential studio, The Manor, in Oxfordshire. Keren and I accompanied them and were thrilled to find ourselves residing in a gorgeous house with a swimming pool. While the band were recording, we spent most of our time careering around the pool in rubber dinghies or playing with the Irish wolfhounds who were running amok in the grounds. When dinner was served, we all sat around a large table in a cosy kitchen with Richard Branson. It was all wholly unreal. One day we heard the roar of a motorbike tearing up the gravel drive. It was Lemmy from Motörhead, who was surprisingly sweet, and his girlfriend, Motorcycle Irene, who terrified us on sight: all leather and fishnets, with long red hair and a supremely confident swagger.

—

KEREN: We'd met Lemmy before, as he was often at The Music Machine in Camden Town, where we frequently went with Paul and Steve. He was usually pleasant, but once playfully threw me over the bar, which was a bit of a shock. That was in the days before The Music Machine became the trendier and more glamorous Camden Palace. It was more of a rock/New Wave venue back then, where bands like Bauhaus, Echo and the Bunnymen and The Cure played. Sometimes, it was noticeably rough, like the occasion when an angry-faced bloke stubbed his cigarette out on my neck because I was served before him. As you can imagine, that was quite horrifying.

We continued to boil a kettle when we needed a wash, occasionally scraping 50p together for a bath at the Oasis swimming pool in Covent Garden. Most days we went to the Gioconda cafe in Denmark Street for breakfast. The fact that it had been a regular haunt of many musicians, including David Bowie, gave it some added glamour that maybe the premises were lacking – a bit like going into Bar Italia on Frith Street for a coffee, you felt like you were soaking up a bit of history. We existed on chips and beans, sometimes splashing out on greasy Kentucky Fried Chicken breasts, with that delicious secret ingredient. It was there that we got chatting to a group of skinheads, a few weeks after we'd moved into the office. They told us they were recording at a studio in Denmark Street, where David Bowie, John Lennon, Jimi Hendrix, The Rolling Stones and others had previously worked, and they invited us along to what became our first experience of singing in a recording studio. It was a rather raucous rendition of 'Stand By Me', with Sara and I singing backing vocals. We recorded into the early hours, but I don't think the recording ever saw the light of day.

—

SARA: I'm not sure how long Keren and I lived in Denmark Street, with its leaky roof and plastic bags pinned up on the ceiling to catch the drips. It was probably about six months. It's funny, we had nothing but it didn't seem to matter. We were having the most fantastic time. Keren was still working at the BBC and, after I'd finished college, I would hang out with Mel, an East End girl from Bethnal Green, who I'd met through Siobhan. We were as thick as thieves for a while; she was always hysterical, she just had 'funny bones'. Mel had a young daughter called Joss and her mum, Jo, ran The Britannia pub, off Roman Road. As time went on, Jo took Keren and me under her wing, and we spent many a happy time in the bosom of their family having Sunday lunches with Nanny Glad, who loved a drop of Malibu and often sported leather trousers. Mel's dad, Mick, took me, Mel and her brothers to the races. We piled into the back of his open-top truck and headed to Ascot, stopping at Harrods on the way to pick up hampers of champagne and strawberries. There were quiz nights and competitions galore at The Britannia, and Keren ended up with the accolade of being crowned the pub's champion beer drinker of 1982.

When we weren't hanging out at The Britannia, Mel would travel up to Denmark Street, announcing herself by singing the Snow White trill, 'la, la, la, la, la', at the bottom of the stairs. There, we'd recount our antics from the previous night before heading up Oxford Street to the BBC – occasionally on roller skates – for the subsidised lunch. The bar/restaurant area was always rammed and full of cigarette smoke, and we knew practically everyone in there.

We loved living in Soho but the winter in Denmark Street was harsh. We had some sort of fan heater, but our mattresses ended up damp, and our clothes were damp. It was all pretty grim. Fortunately, our luck was about to change. At some point during our time at the YWCA, Keren had had the presence of mind to put our names down on the council waiting list. When the housing officers visited us in Denmark Street, we instantly racked up so many points we were propelled to the top of the list and pretty soon afterwards we were told there was a flat available for us on the eleventh floor of a tower block just off Theobalds Road, Holborn.

—

KEREN: Siobhan and her boyfriend were sharing a flat with two other girls in Wardour Street, Soho, and we knew they were looking for somewhere else to live so we asked them if they wanted to move in with us. It seemed sensible as the flat had three bedrooms and this way we could split the rent four ways instead of two. They jumped at the offer then promptly insisted on the biggest room because there were two of them.

Of course, we had no money so the place was furnished with knock-off equipment bought from a dodgy local man and a load of old tat from second-hand furniture stores. Our friend Andy had a van and helped us pick up a garish yellow floral seventies sofa from Willesden Green that was stuffed with poly-styrene beads, a fire hazard if ever there was one, and to add to the ambience we painted all the woodwork in the lounge burgundy. I think Andy worked for Designers Guild so we probably got the paint at a discount or free.

Despite our iffy interior design, living conditions were a galaxy away from the YWCA and Denmark Street. True, we had to pay rent, but it was cheap, and the place was warm and dry. If the National Lottery had been around in those days, we'd have felt like we'd won it!

—

SARA: To earn a bit of pin money after college Siobhan and I were working a few evenings a week at the Marquee, the music venue on Wardour Street. It was at the Marquee that Keren and I met our Irish boyfriends and it wasn't too long before they also moved into our semi-luxurious flat. This all felt very grown up, setting us on an equal footing with Siobhan, with proper live-in boyfriends.

—

KEREN: Despite the noticeable upgrade in our living conditions, food preparation still wasn't high on our list of priorities and all our cooking was done in an electric frying pan, which Sara had acquired from a jumble sale. I'm not even sure we had a cooker but I do remember we once tried to heat a saucepan over a mini-bonfire we'd constructed in another pan, on top of the kitchen worktop. It didn't heat anything but did melt the Formica. We had a fridge and a larder, with our own designated shelves in each, but most of our cutlery, utensils, cleaning products and even toilet roll was 'acquired' from various studios, or, once we were signed, from the record company. The lift was often out of action, which meant lugging washing back from the launderette up eleven floors. This was a pain but getting stuck in a lift was my worst nightmare. One day I heard panicked shouting and discovered Mel and Vaughn Toulouse, our good friend who was lead singer in the group Department S, peering through a small crack where the doors of the lift had opened, even though it hadn't yet reached the floor. After that, walking seemed the safer option. I've hated getting into lifts ever since.

With the three of us, plus our boyfriends, the Irish contingent, there were always extra guests in the flat. You wouldn't recognise the place if there wasn't somebody sleeping on the sofa. One night it was Shane MacGowan from The Pogues – I think he was seeing Mel at the time. We'd all piled back to ours after a night at our new local, The Rugby on Lamb's Conduit Street, and he'd completely conked out. The boys drew a cat's nose and whiskers on him with an indelible marker pen. Poor Shane left the next morning with their artwork intact. We saw quite a bit of him in those days although, unsurprisingly, he never ventured back to the flat.

—

SARA: Most nights, after Siobhan and I finished work at the Marquee, the entire gang would go to a club opposite. The St Moritz was frequented by just about every misfit and musician London had to offer. It was run by a Swede, who was, somewhat unimaginatively, known as Sweedy. He kept a six-foot-long Swiss mountain horn behind the bar, which, on occasion, he'd blow for no particular reason, and whenever he slipped into the back for five minutes, we'd grab the chance to help ourselves to free drinks. It was always such a fun place to hang out, and we'd dance the night away to Michael Jackson's *Off the Wall* and other disco classics.

—

KEREN: The flat was always full of music too. After a night out at The Rugby we'd have regular sing-songs, bashing out our takes of 'I Could Have Danced All Night' and 'Night Fever'. Everyone would jump on whatever instruments were to hand – guitars, bodhráns (Irish drums), even recorders, which Sara was a master on. And my favourite, a Yamaha keyboard. I'm not sure where it came from, but I used my classical training to significant effect, even though there was no need as it was one of those machines that had a slot-in card that played backing tracks with drums, so all I had to play was a top-line melody.

—

SARA: The flat in Holborn was really the genesis of Bananarama. Siobhan and I were both dating musicians who had previously been in bands and my boyfriend was putting a new one together called The Adventures. The whole vibe of what they were doing seemed exciting, so in the spirit of adventure, we decided to have a go. We each bought a Dictaphone to warble our early attempts at songwriting into. Meanwhile, I asked Paul if we could use Denmark Street to try a few of the ideas out. Together with Paul, my boyfriend Terry and various musician friends, the three of us – Siobhan, Keren and myself – rehearsed 'Aie a Mwana' and 'Venus'.

—

KEREN: It was the post-punk era and the 'get up and have a go' ethos remained. The Wag, which was started by Chris Sullivan and Ollie O'Donnell in 1982, was a club for non-conformists. It had a night called Club Left and was the first place we ever performed as Bananarama. It became our essential 'go to' club over the next few years.

Wearing polka-dot catsuits and with elaborately

backcombed hair, we'd jump up on stage and perform a couple of Frank Sinatra numbers with Vic Godard and Subway Sect as our backing band, with our good friend Spud singing the Frank parts with his lovely husky voice. We had a regular slot singing 'Something Stupid' and 'High Hopes', then we finished by belting out 'Aie a Mwana' over a backing track on cassette.

—

SARA: As things were progressing, a friend of ours organised a meeting with Bernie Rhodes, who'd managed The Clash, at Marine Ices in Camden. We saw him as a potential manager, but he suggested we go underground for a year to learn our craft. A year seemed a lifetime so he was immediately rejected. We were young and full of energy, and we certainly had no time to waste. So we approached future DJ and presenter Gary Crowley, who, at the time, was dating Siobhan's sister. Gary worked for a music company called MultiMedia and he introduced us to Clive Banks, who ran it.

—

KEREN: Our meeting with Clive was a success and he committed to paying for us to record a demo and then license it to an independent label, Demon Records. The MultiMedia offices were on Parker Street in Covent Garden, around the corner from what had once been The Blitz club and was now Brown's. We went there most days to visit Gary or to hang out in the basement studio with Siobhan's friends from her school days in

Hertfordshire, Pete Barrett and Nick Egan, who created artwork for upcoming bands. (Years later, Nick directed the video for our single, 'Long Train Running'.)

—

SARA: We spent hours in their office and one of my abiding memories is of listening to Duran Duran's first single, 'Planet Earth', which they played constantly. It was during this period that we got to know Clive's secretary, Hillary Shaw – who later became our manager – as well as Fachtna O'Kelly who managed The Boomtown Rats out of the same building.

Paul arranged for us to record a demo of 'Aie a Mwana' in Shepherd's Bush, where Pete Overend Watts, who was a member of the seventies rock band Mott the Hoople, had a studio. Paul played drums and helped produce the track. I'd first heard the song when I'd visited Siobhan in her Soho flat. She was playing the original version, recorded by Black Blood and sung in Swahili, while eating scrambled egg from a teacup. We all liked the song, and learned the lyrics phonetically, with only the vaguest idea of what we were singing about. It now seems like a peculiar choice for a first recording. I believe it got to number ninety-two in the charts.

—

KEREN: The vocal booth was a tight squeeze with all three of us crammed inside but nothing could take away the fact that this was a massively exciting day. At least it was until Siobhan knocked her cup of tea over the mixing desk and various studio bods started shouting at us. Typically, we didn't think it a big deal and managed to get all the recording done, despite the loss of a few channels. At the end of a long recording session, we were all thrilled with the results. We sounded rather good, even in Swahili!

——

SARA: Our friend Vaughn Toulouse gave us our first foray onto an actual stage at a proper live music venue, singing backing vocals for his band, Department S, on a cover of T. Rex's 'Solid Gold Easy Action'. Siobhan was on holiday at the time so Mel stepped in. Vaughn was a good friend of Paul Weller, which was how we later ended up

With Vaughn Toulouse in Brighton.

supporting The Jam at the Michael Sobell Sports Centre. Paul was keen on promoting new talent and I imagine we just sang a couple of songs as part of a showcase but I still remember his fans pelting us with coins. Later he ended up writing a song for our first album.

—

KEREN: Shy as we all were, we grabbed every opportunity to step into the spotlight, jumping onto the stage whenever there was an opportunity. We shook maracas for The Monochrome Set and sang backing vocals on 'Step On' (later recorded by the Happy Mondays) with The Tea Set. Fronted by Nick Egan, they were friends of Siobhan's and we were really thrilled because not only were we playing at legendary music venue, The Rainbow, but Iggy Pop was headlining. Sara and I played his album *The Idiot* countless times as teenagers at home and at the hostel.

—

SARA: Once we'd recorded our demo, we hawked the tape around, performing at various clubs in London: The Embassy, The Rock Garden in Covent Garden, Moonlight in West Hampstead. That's what you did in those days if you wanted to get noticed. We'd have three mics set up on the stage, and as the trumpeting intro to the song started, my heart would race and then we'd skip out onto the stage. We'd jig around singing our Swahili song, occasionally shaking maracas or banging tambourines. As far as I can remember, we went down a storm; we certainly got some nice little reviews in the *Melody Maker* and the *NME*. Eventually, there was a little buzz about us on the London scene, so much so that Clive Banks and Hillary brought Bruce Springsteen down to the Embassy Club to see us. I'm not sure what he made of us, especially as, by that time, we'd enlisted three male friends to join us on stage to do some 'gimpy' dancing.

—

KEREN: By now, we were keen and raring to go, but in our eagerness to get everything moving, we were completely unconcerned with money and had no idea about how the music business worked. We were all just excited to be making a record. Consequently the contract we signed with Demon Records for 'Aie a Mwana' didn't include any advance whatsoever. To be honest, I think we'd been signed as some sort of novelty act.

Before the single's release, Clive called us in and said we had to think of a name for the band or we would be called The Pineapple Chunks. Sara and Mel came up with Bananarama, which was a twist on the Roxy Music song, Pyjamarama mixed with bananas, as the single had a tropical feel. It sounded very catchy to all of us at the time, but obviously, we had no idea that it would last for as long as it has.

Not long after its release, 'Aie a Mwana' got a spin on the hallowed John Peel show on BBC Radio 1, and we all sat excitedly around the radio to listen in. It was quite a moment, hearing ourselves coming over the airwaves. It made everything feel real ... as if Bananarama were truly off and running.

5
TOWER BLOCKS AND *TOP OF THE POPS*

KEREN: Our first photoshoot was with Derek Ridgers, who had a reputation for capturing social scenes and club culture. We went to Brighton and he shot us mucking around in the sea in the polka-dot catsuits Siobhan had picked up while she was on holiday, and on the pier in our second-hand shirts and trousers and current favourite choice of footwear – moccasins. The resulting shots featured Siobhan and me with our root perms and the three of us scowling.

—

SARA: Somehow one of the photos ended up in the *NME*, and another in the fashion bible, *The Face*. And, as it turned out, Terry Hall, ex-frontman of The Specials, also favoured moccasins. When he spotted our picture in the *NME*, he apparently took a shine to us. Indeed, Terry later said in an interview that he 'liked our shoes', and, more importantly, had bought our single after hearing it on John Peel's show, where he championed new artists. This prompted his management to contact Clive Banks to set up a meeting between Terry and us in the Parker Street offices.

It was quite an awkward meeting, with the three of us sitting shyly on the sofa, while Terry sat on the chair opposite, his teacup rattling while we hid behind our fringes. The conversation was pretty monosyllabic. But the upshot was that Terry had formed a new group, Fun Boy Three, with Lynval Golding and Neville Staple from The Specials, and he wanted to ask if we would sing on their debut album. Once the initial excitement of the offer evaporated, we went into a panic, worried that he'd thought we were professional session singers. We needn't have worried. Terry, Lynval and Neville were utterly inclusive from the start and being in the studio, watching them putting tracks together, turned out to be a great learning experience. That said, I was mortified when I pulled out a tube of Rolos and offered one to Terry, only to realise I was offering him a Tampax. He politely declined.

The recording sessions had a DIY feel that seemed fresh and relaxed. As well as singing, they got us playing all kinds of percussion instruments, with each of us on a drum working out the rhythms together.

—

KEREN: 'Aie a Mwana' might have only reached number ninety-two but now it was 1982, and Fun Boy Three were about to release 'It Ain't What You Do (It's the Way

That You Do It),' featuring Bananarama! A follow-up to their brilliant debut, 'The Lunatics Have Taken Over the Asylum'.

Now we had another photoshoot to do and a music video to film. We were comfortable and confident about our style and wanted to wear our own clothes for the photos. In fact, I wore a jumper I'd happily wear now, which I bought at Portobello Market. But the video was something else entirely. We had a make-up artist who made all three of us look exactly the same, even though we have very different faces. I'm not sure it suited any of us, let alone all of us. It certainly didn't work for me. I had a fat face and the make-up artist's wanton abuse of blusher left me looking like an ugly china doll.

On top of that, we were given clothes to wear: those now-famous jersey rah-rah skirts. People never fail to bring those up, as if we'd started some sort of craze. The truth was, those skirts were foisted upon us, and they were certainly not of our choosing.

The video was shot over one very long day, finishing in the freezing cold early hours. At one point, Sara was in a flimsy pink nylon nightdress and black boots, wandering around the top of a building site, in some sort of dream-sequence where she had to pretend-kiss Neville from the Fun Boys. I suppose we'd all imagined that a three-minute pop video wouldn't take all that long to film. It was three minutes, for God's sake! Of course, this was something we were going to have to get used to. That, and the hanging around at TV stations, radio stations, airports and dressing rooms. All that stuff has always been much more draining than the actual work. Even now, my heart sinks when I cast my eyes over some of the backstage facilities provided for the artists at various festivals. Where is the glamour in portaloos and Portakabins, pray tell?

When 'It Ain't What You Do' became a hit, our new life began. Aside from the radio and magazine interviews, there were the uncomfortable early performances on *Top of the Pops*, with us wearing the aforementioned grey rah-rah skirts and moccasins, looking shifty and awkward. We shuffled from side to side, lip-synching to the track, just as everyone did on *Top of the Pops* back in the day. Sara and I had not long left school, and here we were, performing on what had been the most influential TV show of our young lives.

We had no clue which camera we were supposed to be looking at, so Sara and I spent much of the performance glancing sideways at one other. To be fair, Terry Hall didn't exactly exude pizzazz or confidence either, and he was far more experienced than we were. He invariably performed with his natural shyness and brooding disposition firmly on display, which is one of the things I loved about him. He's one of those characters who doesn't say a lot, but it's always worth it when he does.

Sara and I have bumped into the Fun Boys a few times over the years: backstage at a few festivals and gigs. My favourite time was when we ran into Terry at a nightclub in Soho, and took him on a wild rickshaw race to another club while he was squashed between

Youth in a Booth, age 12–17.

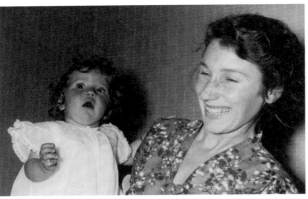

Little cherub Sara with her mother Margaret *(top left)*. Sara, her siblings Paul and Lindsey with their mum on a visit to Symonds Yat in the Wye Valley, Herefordshire *(top right)*. Cousin Helen, brother Matt, mother Doreen and Keren on another wet and windy British holiday *(middle left)*. Sara showing early signs of the party girl to come... *(middle right)*. Baby Keren *(below left)*. Keren and cousins on their family holiday to Wales *(below right)*.

Bob's little angel *(left)*. Uncle Mervyn, cousin Lesley and Sara with her father, Reg *(above)*. Keren in her Sunday Best crimplene dress with her brother, Matt *(below left)*. Sara and her sister, Lindsey, off to a fancy dress party *(below middle)*. Keren and Matt on the rocks *(below right)*.

Happy days in the dunes *(above left)*.
Christmas treats with Paul *(above right)*.
Carefree family holidays in Hampshire
(left/below right). Gina and Keren, Queens
of Corduroy at Windsor Castle *(below left)*.

Perms delight in the Isle of Wight *(top left)*. Disco days with good friends, Sally and Sarah *(top right)*. Teenage kicks, Matt's bedroom *(above left)*. School days *(above middle)*. Platforms, flares and feathercuts *(above right)*. Early beach photoshoot *(right)*.

When peroxide goes wrong at
the YWCA *(above left)*. Sara's
famous kingfisher-blue suit
from Topshop *(above right)*.
Studio 21 *(left)*. Hanging out
with David Bowie *(bottom)*.

Opposite: When peroxide
goes white at the YWCA
(above left). The glamour of
the YWCA accompanied by
a rather unusual look *(above
right)*. Hostel Hair *(below left)*.
Hard girls *(below right)*.

Rock 'n' Roll swindle style at home in Denmark St *(above and left)*. BBC lunch break with Mel O'Brien *(below left)*. Paul Cook and Sara at the Manor *(below right)*.

Sara turns 21 *(top left)*. Cannes in the sand *(top right)*. First trip to NYC filming *Cruel Summer*, 1984 *(above left)*. Drinks with Bob De Niro *(above right)*. TV in the South of France *(below)*.

Shot by the iconic Herb Ritts in LA, 1987 *(above left)*. Matthew Rolston, Bananarama, Group Portrait, 1986 (Courtesy Fahey/Klein, Los Angeles) *(above right)*. A favourite shoot with Jonathan Root, 1987 *(below)*.

Having our fortunes told in Tokyo, Japan *(above left)*. Quick burger stop in Harajuku *(above right)*. Land of the Rising Sun *(right)*. The Wag Club with Chris Sullivan, Stephen Mahoney and Mel O'Brien *(below left)*. The charming Dick Clark, *American Bandstand*, LA *(below right)*.

Last performance with Siobhan, The Brit Awards, 1988 and what a performance! *(above left and right and below left)*. With Bruno Tonioli, Baillie Walsh and Paul Cavalier in Montreux, Switzerland *(below right)*.

(opposite, top to bottom) Party at the Hard Rock Cafe with Rodney Bingenheimer, LA. Keeping it professional on the US promo tour. The mother of all parties on the MTV boat with Andy Warhol, NYC, 1986.

VODKA! Newcastle nightclub.

Our second home, The Sunset Marquis Hotel in LA

us under a blanket. We thought it was a scream, but I'm not sure how much poor Terry enjoyed the experience.

—

SARA: Though somewhat awkward, our appearance on *Top of the Pops* propelled us into the public eye. There was more promotional work, with one of our first TV appearances being on the iconic kids' TV show *Tiswas*, hosted by Chris Tarrant, Lenny Henry and Sally James. Michael Palin was also on that week, and I remember being awed by being on a show with one of the *Monty Python* team. Just before the show, the record company sent us out to buy new outfits and we dashed to the nearest shop. Peter Robinson stood where NIKE Town is now in Oxford Circus. We emerged with striped grey-and-white tunics with matching slim trousers and performed in bare feet. It was a shocking look, and the three of us still laugh about it now.

After that, the promo went international. We were to fly to Amsterdam, no less, for a TV performance. This news brought about a frenzy of excitement, mainly because neither Keren nor I had ever been on a plane before. We'd only been abroad once, for a school trip to Brittany in France and that was on the ferry. I was only eleven at the time, and my principal memories of that excursion were being served a triangular pile of grey bones, which turned out to be a fish called skate, and also acquiring a fourteen-year-old pen pal named Bruno, who later terrified the life out of me by declaring his love for me in a letter.

This trip was to be something else entirely. For a start, Amsterdam seemed so much cooler than Brittany, and we were flying. During take-off, the speed of the plane thundering along the runway thrust our heads back in our seats, and we beamed with excitement. We were staying in a five-star hotel and were utterly thrilled with our gorgeous room, which had a double bed with crisp white sheets. On top of that, we were showered with free clothes, food and drink, and were chauffeur-driven to beautiful restaurants where we had the best nights out with Terry and the boys.

Despite the newness of the lifestyle, the three of us got into the swing of it quickly, although Keren over-indulged at one point and ended up vomiting into the waste-paper bin in her bedroom. Out of the traps too quick, or as Gary Crowley used to say, 'She took the torch and ran out of the stadium.'

Those European TV appearances with the Fun Boys were always hilarious. Lynval and Neville would leap around energetically, bombing about the stage, which was a good distraction from the remaining four of us, who tended to shuffle around while occasionally muttering amusing asides to one another.

On our return to London there was more good news. The buzz about Bananarama was such that we were offered a one-off singles deal with Decca (later London) Records. Not an album – clearly, nobody had a tremendous amount of faith in three young women achieving anything more than a momentary snippet of success – but we weren't going to let that deter us. We took their singles deal and ran with it.

—

KEREN: The Fun Boys wanted to return the favour of us singing on their record by singing on our second single, 'Really Saying Something', a cover of the Motown song originally recorded by The Velvelettes. We gave it the same treatment as 'It Ain't What You Do', with us and the Fun Boys all playing various instruments and Terry and I sitting side by side to play the piano parts.

The video was brighter and more colourful than the one for 'It Ain't What You Do', with a pop-art, cartoon feel, but it was hardly what one would describe as big budget. Still, the record was a hit, reaching number five in the UK, and making it our second Top Five record; 'It Ain't What You Do' had peaked at number four. The difference was that we weren't guesting on somebody else's song. 'Really Saying Something' was a Bananarama record.

—

SARA: Some years later, we met Madonna after her LA show on her Virgin Tour and she said she'd loved 'Really Saying Something', and always danced to it at the club Danceteria in New York.

—

KEREN: It was a whirlwind that none of us saw coming. I'd left the BBC to give this pop thing a go but financially it wasn't happening at all. There was this short but weird period when all three of us were signing on the dole while simultaneously gracing the nation's television screens, with everyone thinking we'd hit the big time. But we still hadn't had an advance, and there was no money in the pipeline. Sure, the record company had picked up an album option with us, which they were paying for us to record, but we had nothing to live on. Something had to change and fast.

We urgently needed help and decided to take Fachtna O'Kelly on as our manager. He arranged for us to get a £5,000 bank loan, and out of that, we paid ourselves £40 per week. It wasn't too bad. The rent on our flat amounted to about £14 a week each, so that was a whole twenty-six quid left over for everything else. Fachtna also advised us to get lawyers, introducing us to Tony Russell and Chris Organ – Chris still represents us today. Chris was quite newly qualified when we first started working together. He calls us the ravens in his tower and insists the day we stop or leave him is the day he will retire! Whenever we have meetings, we try to time them for late morning so afterwards we can head out for a long lunch together in Soho. Tony and Chris immediately set about negotiating a fairer deal for us, although in those days, the recording studio costs were so astronomical, it was never easy to recoup any advances. I never really followed all the figures, but we have a multitude of silver, gold and even platinum discs so I guess we did OK.

Once our album deal was signed, we were offered a

publishing deal, worth about £5,000. That seemed like a fortune to Sara and I and we were keen to sign, but Siobhan suggested we wait. Having worked for Decca Records and knowing a bit more about how the business worked, her thinking was that after we'd had a couple more hits, we could get much more than that. Our lawyers, Tony and Chris, agreed, and thank God we listened to them and waited another six months to sign. The financial difference in our publishing worth by then was colossal.

—

SARA: Things started to snowball, moving faster than we ever could have imagined. I'm not sure anyone knew exactly where the train was heading but it was clear that people wanted to be on it – just in case Bananarama did turn out to be something big. We were still quite inexperienced so we worked the only way we knew how – by instinct. We were young and we loved clubbing and on nights out we started to make all kinds of fascinating and useful creative acquaintances: people in fashion, art and of course music. As a band we started writing our own material and used some of our new friends to design artwork for us, while we made our own clothes. We may not have had any money, but everything about us was authentic.

Some of our TV interviews of the time remain hilarious, and occasionally painful to watch. Still pretty shy despite our success, when we did deign to speak, it was in high-pitched voices with mockney accents.

Rather than jumping in to answer a question, we'd all just look at one another, all desperate for somebody else to speak. Whoever was nearest to the interviewer and unlucky enough to have to answer would glance at the other two for reassurance, and then we'd all start giggling. We loved music and writing songs, but the idea of selling the finished product was utterly alien to us.

Bananarama had a fabulous press officer in the late Eugene Manzi, who we had so much fun hanging out with. Still, there wasn't much advice from the label on how we should be conducting ourselves in interviews or on television, so we generally just hid behind our hair. It's not like the three of us were dim – we had armfuls of O- and A-levels between us – but there was

How to achieve Bananarama hair – no glam squad necessary.

nothing in our armoury to help us deal with fame and the wonderful world of showbiz at such a young age. We had to learn in the public eye as we went along. There was no media training. Nobody sat us down and said, 'OK, they're going to discuss this. These are the questions, and you might want to answer like this.' Instead, we were simply pushed out onto the ice, spontaneous and natural, which sometimes read as shy and awkward.

When I look back at those early TV interviews, I remember how anxious I was in some of them. Sometimes the interviewer would make you feel worthy, and other times, merely token and unimportant.

A few years later, I remember watching some of the young pop acts of the early nineties being interviewed, so confident and sure of themselves. I realised that quite a few of them had been to stage school, but I'm not sure even that would have helped us, because none of us possessed that kind of personality. Wham! were always viewed as bright, bubbly boys, back in the day, but in interviews they were as inexperienced as we were, and also guilty of 'mockney'. Thinking about it, a lot of bands tended to speak that way during that period. Perhaps it was the thing.

—

While we struggled with the interviews, we really enjoyed appearing on *Top of the Pops*, and for a while, it seemed like we were on it every week. There was such a buzz around doing that show back in the eighties. All the acts who appeared on any particular week would invariably end up in the BBC bar – before and after the recording. That was always the best fun. Aside from hanging out with our contemporaries, we found ourselves mingling with bands and artists that we'd grown up watching on the show. Seeing Led Zeppelin in the bar after filming one night was particularly memorable. I later did a TV *Pop Quiz* with Robert Plant as my team captain.

It was 1982 and suddenly we were being flown off to Europe, America, Australia and Japan – often being flown long-haul in economy, before we knew better! It was all so exciting and Japan was a wonderful culture shock, unlike anything any of us had ever experienced. Tokyo felt like a dream world from the minute you stepped off the plane: the architecture, the gadgets, the food, the people and, of course, the shopping. I was fascinated by the contrast between the old culture and customs of the country – with traditional meals, clothes and temples – and the craziest fashion areas, like Harajuku and Shibuya and the street performers and bands in Yoyogi Park. There was neon everywhere you turned, and I felt like I'd stepped into a futuristic movie, full of exciting new technology. The Japanese seemed to have a similar sense of humour to us and the record company and translators who accompanied us on our travels were great fun and the perfect hosts.

I remember one particularly beautiful restaurant in a gorgeous Japanese garden, complete with mini waterfalls and streams. We had to change into wooden platform clogs to walk through it before sitting cross-legged on the floor at our table. After dinner, we'd go to clubs and dance all night. The lovely translator, Yas, had to stay with us no matter what, so if we wanted to dance until five in the morning, she had to stay too. Japanese nightlife was so varied – from tiny bars and karaoke haunts to state-of-the-art nightclubs and drag shows, where we caught a performance of some drag queens covering our single 'Movin' On' a few years later. Everybody who came to Tokyo went to the club Lexington Queen. Run by the fabulous, larger-than-life Bill Hersey, it was our favourite place. Drinks were on the house all night, though he'd always herald our arrival by shining a huge spotlight on us as the DJ cued

Lunch at the lake, Tokyo.

up 'Venus', just in case we were planning on slipping in quietly. Photos of celebrities lined the corridors and, years later when showing some friends around the club, having mentioned we'd been a few times, we were shocked to see just how many times. There were numerous shots of us in black wigs, blond wigs and with arms around fellow pop stars.

The shopping was like nothing else. Huge, eight-storey buildings with the most creative fashion I'd ever seen on each floor, while the little back streets teemed with a mixture of Western, vintage and high-street clothes. Vivienne Westwood's clothes were really popular there and still are. We'd always return home with suitcases full of clothes: Yamamoto, and Comme des Garçons, and original 1950s Levi's with the red stitched seams, and other vintage finds. The clothes would become part of our promotional look for the upcoming single releases. The bottle-green velvet suit I'm wearing on the cover of 'Venus' came from Tokyo and I'm pretty sure Siobhan's dress and Keren's black wig were from there too.

—

KEREN: It didn't matter where we'd been in the world, we'd always head to The Wag as soon as we were back in London. One night when Sara and I had just flown back from a holiday in Greece, we dashed home, threw our cases in the door and, after pulling on some leather trousers, ran straight out. Having sweated so much while I was dancing, by the time I got home I somehow managed to peel off a week's worth of suntan along with the trousers.

—

SARA: Another time when we were there, we heard a song called 'Body Talk' by Imagination. It was such a slinky track with a great baseline. The next day, we were on a mission to find out who had produced this fantastic piece of pop-funk, and then to ask if they'd be up for working on some tracks with us. Enter Steve Jolley and Tony Swain, and a whole new musical chapter.

6

GOOD MORNING, AMERICA

SARA: I don't know what Steve and Tony made of us on our first meeting, or what preconceived ideas they may have had about a modern-day girl group, but it didn't take long for them to get the gist. When we arrived at Red Bus Studios in Marylebone, they presented us with a song called 'Big Red Motorbike', which we rejected immediately as we weren't keen on the lyrics. They had written a girly Motownesque song, I guess figuring that's what we'd want, given our predecessors had been the likes of The Ronettes, The Supremes and the other Motown girl groups of the sixties. But although we were fans of those groups, we weren't trying to emulate them. After a rewrite, 'Big Red Motorbike' eventually became 'Shy Boy' and our next Top Five hit.

We were blown away when we received a congratulatory telegram from Paul and Linda McCartney. Subsequently, we were invited to a few of Linda's photographic exhibitions and both she and Paul were always so down to earth and friendly. Linda sent us demos

What a moment! Meeting Paul and Linda McCartney, with Mel
O'Brien (right).

of songs we might like to listen to, which was amazing. It
felt great to have a successful woman encouraging and
supporting us while we were just starting our careers.

We performed 'Shy Boy' at the BRITs, with a rather
unusual dance routine. I don't recall who brought a
choreographer in but I imagine the record company
thought it might help with the performance. It didn't.
The routine, complete with us leapfrogging over each
other in checked lumberjack shirts with braces holding
up second-hand men's suit trousers, was not our finest
moment, particularly given the lack of conviction that's
apparent in the execution of it.

Our journey with Jolley and Swain was a joy; we
had so much fun in the recording studio. They were

both brilliant songwriters, so working with them was inspirational. What they taught us about constructing and arranging a song, harmonies and hook lines was invaluable. They also appreciated our creativity and listened to our ideas. Of course, we wanted to write lyrics from the point of view of the young women we were, and they saw the importance of that. With that in mind, we agreed to co-write everything and set about creating our first album, *Deep Sea Skiving*. The album features one of my earliest attempts at songwriting. I wrote the lyrics to 'What a Shambles', a song about our newfound fame and the juxtaposition of doing promo while still having to cart our clothes to the launderette.

I was proud of it at the time, and smile when I hear it now, because I remember so clearly how put-upon I felt. Another early attempt at honing our songwriting skills was 'Boy Trouble', which the three of us loved. The journalist, Julie Burchill, gave that particular song a favourable mention in her review of the album. In those days, records had B-sides, which we always enjoyed writing. There was 'Scarlett', 'Girl About Town' and 'Cairo', which we recorded with reggae star Dennis Bovell, and also 'Give Us Back Our Cheap Fares', which was a protest song about the rise in Tube fares. Bizarrely, that one had no lyrics. Just the title statement. We had so much freedom to write whatever we wanted, there was no pressure.

—

KEREN: I've always loved working in a studio on bringing a song to life. The way layering vocals and harmonies on a track can enhance a song has always thrilled me, and I learned from 'The Master', which was what we always called Steve Jolley. Sara and I have carried what we learned from Steve throughout our career. On the odd occasion we've experimented by recording a song without embellishments but for me it's just not Bananarama when we do. We're all about the harmonies and counter-melodies, and luckily, we both have an ear for them. Sara loves to throw in the odd 'down-in-her-boots' low harmony during live shows, particularly during 'Nathan Jones'. I ought to be prepared for its arrival by now, but it always reduces me to a choking mess, to the point where I struggle to get my next line out.

Although Tony and Steve were very different people, they worked wonderfully together. Steve had a talent for both melody and unusual lyrical ideas and always looked like he'd just stepped out of an army training session, with his shaved head and combat trousers. Tony was much more conventionally turned out and created inventive musical backing tracks, which always supported the vocals with what we called the 'Swain Sustain', a signature sound that featured in the productions they did for Imagination, Spandau Ballet and my favourite of theirs, *Alf* by Alison Moyet.

During these early recording sessions, uncontrollable giggling in the studio would, on occasion, see us sent out to take a breather. Back then, Siobhan, Sara and I mostly sang around the same microphone, or in small glass booths next to each other. It wasn't always easy, particularly

given Siobhan's penchant for beef and onion sandwiches and belching. Back then, catching one another out of the corner of an eye was enough to set us all off giggling, and although our producers were generally tolerant, occasionally it all got too much for them.

We recorded some of *Deep Sea Skiving* at Utopia Studios in Primrose Hill with seventies pop star and songwriter, Barry Blue, where I also had a game of pool with Sting. We were obsessed with the board game Frustration, which, as you'll know if you've ever played it, is very difficult to play quietly. We'd play between takes but however hard we tried being gentle with the 'Pop-o-Matic' dice device, we always managed to make a noise and piss everyone off. During another session, Tony Swain sent us packing from Red Bus Studios after one too many attempts to sing a single line without laughing. If one of us managed to get the line out, the others did not. And this went on for some time. Tony told us to come back when we'd grown up, like a frustrated parent with the recording studio version of the naughty step.

—

SARA: The three of us were really close at this point, and always cracking up at inappropriate moments. We'd shuffle into rooms for interviews, crushing onto a sofa together, even if there were vacant chairs. This was partly for security, but also so we could make amusing asides to one another, which was something we did on stage and off. It was fortunate that there were three of us because if two of us got a fit of the giggles, the third could pick up the slack. When Siobhan and I had an uncontrollable laughing fit in an interview on Japanese TV, all very juvenile, Keren soldiered gallantly on. Her high-pitched cockney tones struggled under our relentless guffawing.

To be fair, during those early days of promo, we'd often flown halfway around the world with very little sleep. We were talking about ourselves from morning to night, making the same points repeatedly and, being a band of young women, we also did an inordinate number of fashion shoots. This was especially true when we were in Japan. We had hardly any time to ourselves and it could be mentally and physically exhausting, and certainly not conducive to sharpness during our umpteenth interview of the day.

The eighties were a great time to be a pop star. Just as our career started, so did MTV, appearing on TV screens all over the world like some beacon of the future. As an up-and-coming band, we'd featured in *NME*, *Melody Maker* and *The Face*, but as the eighties progressed, so came the rise of glossy pop mags like *Smash Hits* and *No.1*, which became essential reading for any self-respecting teen or pre-teen pop fan.

Some areas of the media seemed to have a preconceived idea of what we were about. Sets of photoshoots were festooned with balloons and streamers. For one tabloid newspaper shoot, we were faced with racks of brightly coloured rah-rah skirts and pastel, candy-striped tops with oversized bows. While it was all a million miles away from who we were, rejecting the ideas made us appear 'awkward' and 'difficult', a criticism that would never have been levelled at our male counterparts.

—

KEREN: When Neil Tennant of Pet Shop Boys interviewed us, in his previous incarnation as a journalist for *Smash Hits*, he admitted to being scared of us because we seemed so stand-offish. People thought we had an attitude. For the most part, we could do our own thing, but there were some uncomfortable moments with early photoshoots. On our first encounter with a stylist, we were presented with a selection of clothes more suited to a Page Three model than a girl band. Still, we were all expected to find something on the rack. Under pressure, we each cobbled together an outfit, utilising the least objectionable garments on the rail. There was one photographer who often worked for the tabloids who bumbled around in Coke-bottle-thick glasses, a doppelgänger for Benny Hill's character Ernie – the fastest milkman in the west. I think he was more used to photographing topless models than young pop stars and suggested horribly out-of-character poses.

'Could you get down on all fours on the fur rug and pretend to be cats?' came one request.

'Don't be ridiculous!' came the answer.

He always knew when he was beaten and despite the sexist connotations of his requests, we had a soft spot for him because he never put us under any pressure.

'You can't blame me for trying,' he'd say.

On those early photoshoots, we laughed off a fair

few of these situations with a resounding group 'NO!' but never considered making an official complaint. It just wasn't something one did back then.

Ultimately, we knew how we wanted to look, and insisted on having our say on make-up, hair and clothes, particularly when it came to the photoshoot for the *Deep Sea Skiving* album cover. The concept was that the three of us were underwater, swimming with fish, while wearing black tunics we'd made on my gran's old sewing machine. The location for the shoot was a studio with an elaborate set. Sara had terrible flu and had loads of tissue stuffed up her T-shirt sleeve, and I had long-johns on under my long skirt and leggings.

—

SARA: I suppose Bananarama was quite challenging for some people: dressing the way we did, writing our own songs, and voicing our opinions, particularly about the way the group was run.

In the advertising industry, the concept of what was expected of a young girl group was even more unpalatable. We were once offered a million dollars to advertise hair tongs in the US, but took one look at the storyboard, with three frilly girls curling their hair in the mirror, and said, 'Thank you, but no!'

We were much keener when we were offered the chance to appear in a Japanese motorbike commercial with Peter Fonda, who'd starred alongside Dennis Hopper and Jack Nicholson in the cult movie *Easy Rider*. The job was set up by a lovely guy called Kaz, a Japanese promoter who loved the British music scene and had already put together some big commercials using Culture Club and Duran Duran. Before we even left London for the shoot, though, a request came through from someone in LA, asking us to send Polaroids of our legs, given we would be riding mopeds. This sexist request didn't amuse us, and Fachtna put his foot down and told them there would be no Polaroids.

It was no real surprise that those kinds of attitudes were still prevalent. So much of what was on television, in prime-time slots, was sexist, racist and homophobic and it took – and is still taking – a long time for people's attitudes to change. We always tried to stand up for ourselves and were lucky in many ways but to trivialise what we sometimes went through doesn't do justice to all those who have helped make change possible or honour the women, in every walk of life, who are still fighting and struggling to achieve equality.

If we gloss over our experiences we wouldn't be playing our part in trying to change women's lives.

—

KEREN: To be fair, while we'd baulked at being asked for photos of our legs, when we were invited to perform at the Miss Hawaiian Tropic pageant, we didn't say no. This was an international beauty contest to find women to serve as spokesmodels for Hawaiian Tropic products. In hindsight, as strong, independent, young women, maybe we shouldn't have been supporting the idea of a contest designed to find spokesmodels for tanning products. But when it came down to it, it was a paid trip to Hawaii with a suite each on the beach. We hobnobbed with country singer Glenn Campbell and Audrey Landers who had played Afton Cooper in *Dallas* and got caught in a violent sandstorm.

—

SARA: Our first trip to California – where we filmed the Japanese motorbike commercial – was everything I'd imagined it would be: sunshine, palm trees, vast freeways, beaches, diners and the legendary Sunset Boulevard. Arriving at LAX, we were ushered into a limo and we made an immediate request that the chauffeur stop at the first available drive-thru McDonald's. This was something we'd only seen in the movies and eventually became a tradition whenever we

With Hillary Shaw in Hawaii.

landed there. The commercial was filmed in the Valley in forty-degree heat, which, at times, was unbearable. Whenever there was a lull in shooting, I'd take off on the bike around the huge parking lot with the sun beating down and the wind in my hair. I was having the time of my life. Peter Fonda was a lovely guy and told me I reminded him of his actress daughter, Bridget.

KEREN: Generally, we were something of a novelty in the States, especially when we appeared on old-school shows like Dick Clark's *American Bandstand*. There we were, on one occasion, with our long, draped, 'cavewomen'-style outfits from Hyper-Hyper in Kensington, and our World's End leggings, looking like nothing the audience had ever seen. Dick Clark was absolutely charming, but even he was very amused by our attire.

—

SARA: In Europe, our style and attitude wasn't quite such an anomaly, but in America, particularly in the southern states, it was as if we were a trio of aliens. It's not like we particularly threatened people; they just seemed to find us amusing. At a music conference in Atlanta, we found ourselves at a pool party which was full of bikini-clad women in hot tubs with music execs and radio DJs. Meanwhile, there we were, sitting on sun loungers fully clothed with our Dr Martens on, in blistering heat. Every so often, the resident DJ would

Such an exciting time performing on *American Bandstand*, LA.

shout out on the mic, 'Hey, Bananarama, strip off and join us in the hot tub!'

Of course, we just looked over, smiled politely and stayed exactly where we were. Despite the general notion that we were a bit odd, America embraced us, and we all loved being there.

—

KEREN: On an early trip to New York, the three of us were taken to the Russian Tea Rooms by the PR from our record company. It was probably the first touristy thing we'd ever done in the city, as much of the time we were just working. While there, we were happily chatting and enjoying the new experience, when a man ambled towards us from the other side of the restaurant.

'Hi, I'm Michael,' he said. 'My daughter is a big fan, and I wonder if you could sign something for her.'

It was Michael bloody Caine!

While trying to remain calm and collected, I was trying to get my head around the fact that Michael Caine was even aware of our existence. As I said, it was early days for us, and back then I suppose we still weren't used to the connotations of fame – that yes, people knew who we were! I'd never been massively starstruck, but Michael Caine was an exception. Not that any of us let it show – we all kept it ridiculously cool. Michael was a proper old-school star, and I doubt he'd made a single film I hadn't watched on TV growing up: *The Ipcress File*, *The Italian Job*, or, my Dad's favourite, *Battle of Britain*. He turned out to be the most charming man.

About ten years later, during the nineties, Sara and I were at a Versace party in Bond Street, trapped with a particularly obnoxious DJ who was showing off while trying to procure Sara's phone number. Just as we were about to wander off in search of someone more interesting to talk to, a man walked over to join us.

'I don't know if you remember me, but we met in New York,' he said.

I wanted to scream, 'Of course we bloody remember you, you're Michael Caine!'

However, I just said a polite 'yes, of course' and 'nice to see you'. Then we stood, chatting for a while. Meeting someone you've put on a pedestal can be disappointing but with Michael, this wasn't the case at all.

After shooting our first few videos in studios and around London, the idea of flying off to shoot the video for our single 'Cheers Then', was a real thrill. We flew to Salzburg in Austria, which was especially exciting as we all adored *The Sound of Music*. The idea was that we would shoot in some of the film's famous locations, recreating scenes from the movie. There were marionettes, bike rides along the river and running around the streets with large stringed instruments in cases.

—

SARA: Meanwhile, the clothes for the video were typically DIY. We'd bought a few metres of heavy wool fabric from the market, and swiftly cut and stitched long, ill-fitting skirts together. Mine and Keren's had no discernible shape and were extremely bulky. We teamed them with cut-off sweatshirts, and we'd saved up for 'Buffalo Girl' hats from Vivienne Westwood's shop, which we were now brave enough to go into.

—

KEREN: It was lots of fun, and I admit to finding a tear in my eye on the odd occasions I've re-watched it. Having a bigger budget for the video, however, didn't necessarily translate into a higher chart position, and after a run of Top Five singles, 'Cheers Then' only reached number forty-five. Although we hadn't expected chart success when we started, we had become accustomed to it and this came as quite a blow, especially as we really loved the song and video. We put it down to the fact that, although it wasn't a traditional ballad, it was a slower song. Our fingers were burned and although we have one slow song on most of the albums we've recorded, we've never since risked releasing one as a single.

'Cheers Then' was also the song we performed on our funniest TV appearance ever, *The Krankies' Christmas Show*. We stood on a mock fire escape – me in a V-neck cable-knitted tank top – as fake snow fell in unnatural clumps in front of us. Towards the end of the song, we descended the steps of the fire escape onto a rooftop set, where we swayed from side to side. It wasn't exactly ambitious choreography but we couldn't even manage that, so when one of us would go one way, the other two would go the other. There's a counter-melody at the end of the song, which we didn't seem to know the words to, so there were several close-ups of confused looks with no one actually miming to the vocals. It was all a bit of a shambles but, I like to think, it was part of the Bananarama charm.

7

FRENCH DISCOS AND TALKING ITALIAN

KEREN: After parting company with Fachtna as a manager, we had a brief period with a guy called Barry Dickens who took over the role. He was an established music agent with an impressive roster of big names past and present. He accompanied us on a trip to LA where we stayed at the Hyatt House on Sunset Boulevard, or 'The Riot House' as it had been known. We were fascinated by his tales of 1970s debauchery, when groups like The Rolling Stones, Led Zeppelin and The Who apparently trashed their rooms and threw televisions out of windows.

—

SARA: By then, however, we felt like we needed looking after on a more personal front. Hillary Shaw – Hills as she was known – had started working as our PA, but eventually the role turned into a managerial one. Hills was kind and caring, looking after us like a surrogate mother, which

was something we all needed. I'm sure managing us couldn't have been the easiest job in the world. She must have wanted to tear her hair out on occasion, trying to keep control of three wayward children. We had some great times together, and although we parted company professionally in the early nineties, Keren and I have remained good friends with her.

By the time Hillary came on board, we were embarking on our second album, *Bananarama*, and were growing in confidence. We'd also really got into the swing of songwriting. 'Cruel Summer' was about all our friends going away on holiday while we were stuck in the city, working. I have fond memories of sitting in the flat in Holborn, writing the lyrics with Siobhan after Steve and Tony had given us the basic backing track to work on. I think it's a great song, and it's special to me as it was our first Top Ten hit in America.

While we were there on tour it was played everywhere we went – the beaches, the diners, the stores and the clubs.

In the early to mid-1980s, college radio stations in the US were essential. These were the stations that tended to break away from the typical mainstream US rock, playing alternative and imported music. 'Cruel Summer' was one such track. It was picked up by DJ Rodney Bingenheimer and played on his massively influential shows at the Los Angeles station KROQ.

I think he'd also been the first US DJ to play 'Really Saying Something' and was a big supporter of the group. We met him on several occasions, both at the station and at social events. It was a joy to talk to someone passionate and knowledgeable about all types of music.

While 'Cruel Summer' was being played on a Los Angeles station one day, the producer of a yet-to-be-released film heard it. He loved the song and asked to use it in *The Karate Kid*. Of course, we said yes, and as luck would have it, we just happened to be in LA when the film was released. We went to the movie's opening night at Grauman's Chinese Theatre, on the Hollywood Walk of Fame. The song was played during the film and at the end, as the credits rolled. The thrill of seeing my name come up on a Hollywood movie while in Hollywood was somewhat awesome.

At one social event, KROQ was broadcasting from the Hard Rock Cafe in LA. We were really excited to discover Joey Ramone in one of the restaurant booths and to finally meet the group after so many years. It was also here that I was scouted by the Ford modelling agency, which certainly did wonders for my confidence.

The second single from our second album was 'Robert De Niro's Waiting'. We'd been working on the song at Steve's house and had been using a drum machine, thinking we wanted it to sound something like Grace Jones's 'Pull Up to the Bumper'. That session had been interrupted by Steve's discovery of a new track, Frankie Goes to Hollywood's 'Relax'. It was an incredible song, and Trevor Horn's production sounded immense. The following week, Steve and Tony came round to our flat and we worked on the song again. We wanted to write about the difficulties of communicating within relationships and the negative experiences; how some girls retreat into a fantasy world where the pop stars and movie stars they had pinned on their bedroom walls were their boyfriends. Keren and I were big fans of De Niro and *The Godfather Part II* had recently been shown again on TV. Most of the guys we knew were obsessed with it, endlessly quoting all the iconic lines, so we decided to use his name.

The final track didn't sound like Grace Jones or Frankie but was a great tune nonetheless and was a big hit. Around the time of the release, De Niro was in London filming Terry Gilliam's movie *Brazil*, and we heard through the grapevine that he wanted to meet us; he had probably been alerted to the track by our mutual PRs. We were all at home one evening, watching

Brookside, when the payphone in the hall rang and my boyfriend Terry answered it. He came rushing into the living room, yelling excitedly.

'Bob De Niro's on the phone and wants to speak to one of you.'

None of us believed him at first, but eventually he sounded convincing enough to send all three of us scuttling to the phone and huddling around the receiver.

We decided Siobhan should speak, but it was pretty monosyllabic from both ends.

Bob: 'Hello!'

Siobhan: 'Hello!'

Bob: 'Do you want to meet for a drink later?'

Siobhan: 'Yeah, all right.'

The respective PRs took it from there, which was probably for the best.

Bob wasn't finished filming until later that evening, so we all rushed to the pub to spread the exciting news that we were going to meet Robert De Niro in Soho that night! This turned out to be a huge mistake, as all our boyfriends wanted to come, as well as some of our friends. In the end, we hatched a plan that they could come and sit in the bar, but they couldn't sit at the same table or let on that they knew us.

We met Bob in Kettner's, in Romilly Street, Soho, which had long been a favourite haunt of ours. The restaurant was founded in 1867 by Napoleon III's chef, Auguste Kettner, and had been frequented by luminaries such as Edward II and his mistress Lillie Langtry, Oscar

Wilde, Agatha Christie and Noël Coward. Now it was going to be the setting for a meeting between Bananarama and the coolest and most esteemed of Hollywood actors.

As we sat by the window, sipping our vodka tonics, with various friends dotted casually around the bar, an unassuming chap in a bobble hat and glasses started tapping at the window, trying to attract our attention. Unfortunately, we didn't recognise Bob in this unexpected get-up and assumed he was some nuisance or an overzealous fan.

When Kettner's closed we moved to Zanzibar, a private members' bar in Covent Garden. All in all, it was a strange evening, sitting there with a Hollywood legend and his producer. Still, the cocktails flowed and we had a great time though the only specific thing I can remember now is Bob inquiring about my trainers and pronouncing Adidas peculiarly. They were in fact Nike, which I was wearing with a raincoat from Oxfam, obviously going all out to impress.

—

KEREN: My memory is of Bob taking a bit of a shine to Sara, telling her she had the sexiest smile he'd ever seen. We all imagined he'd said much the same thing to many a fine woman, but it was a moment.

Around this time, we did two French disco tours, performing twenty-minute sets of our biggest hits in various nightclubs. The tours took us all over France and, while some of these nightspots felt like they were in the

Montreux Music Festival, Switzerland.

middle of nowhere, they were all heaving with people by the time we came on. We ended up in Monte Carlo at the legendary nightclub, Jimmy'z, which was launched in 1974 by the legendary Régine. Jimmy'z was a huge place, with a Japanese garden, known for being totally outrageous and a hangout for the rich and famous. From what I remember, it also had the most expensive bar on earth.

The trips were put together by a promotor called Thierry and were a lot of fun, but at the same time, the set-up of the whole thing was a bit odd. For a start, the money for the shows was all paid in cash, and we had two minder-type guys shadowing us the whole time. We were flown everywhere on a private plane, but when I say private plane, don't for one minute imagine that I'm talking about some swanky, streamlined jet with leather

French disco tour.

seats and onboard champagne cocktails. This thing was a rickety old prop plane; basically, a Cortina with wings. After boarding at Biggin Hill Airfield one afternoon, we were told the plane was too heavy, and we'd have to dump some cargo because it wouldn't take off. We'd brought along some merchandise in the way of T-shirts to sell at the show, and also our boyfriends, so there was a choice to make. In the end, we had to leave the merchandise behind, just so this thing could get off the ground.

—

SARA: On one stop during the tour, we stayed in an old chateau, fitted with the kind of lights that only stay on for a few seconds after you hit the switch. Our rooms were through a door and down a dark corridor full of portraits, with eyes that looked as if they were staring at you. To add to the uneasy atmosphere of the place, the walls in my room were blood red. None of us were all that happy about being there, so we decided it was best if we all stayed together in my room. As Siobhan, Keren and I lounged on my bed chatting, there was a knock at the door. When we answered, in stalked our two brooding security men, who promptly started taking their clothes off. We looked at one another in amazement as the men stripped to their underpants and plonked themselves down on chairs at the end of the bed. There they sat, posing; waiting, one presumed, for us to suggest something. All they got was slightly nervous laughter, which left them totally confused. As they only spoke Italian, communication was limited, but they seemed to get the message. A few moments later, they got up, got dressed and left, totally embarrassed.

—

KEREN: I've thought about that night since and wondered what might have happened if I'd been on my own and two frankly quite scary guys had stripped off without invitation in my hotel room? I'm sure I wouldn't have been laughing then; I'd have been petrified. Having the power of three was a good thing. There was safety in numbers. There were all sorts of occasions back then when 'being three' gave us the wherewithal to manage awkward situations. With hindsight, I can only imagine how tough it must have been for female solo artists. Travelling around the world and doing all that stuff on one's own seems unimaginable, particularly given what was deemed acceptable in those days.

Until we'd got our first publishing deal in 1984, the three of us really didn't have much money. It was quite a change then, to receive an advance that enabled us to leave our council flat and buy our very own houses. Through a friend of Hillary's, Sara, Siobhan and I viewed a row of six or seven brand-new three-storey town houses in Kentish Town, eventually deciding to buy one each. Sara and I were still in our early twenties, so the idea that we were able to buy a house outright was nothing short of incredible, especially when I thought about my parents, who were still paying off their twenty-five-year mortgage. Siobhan chose a slightly bigger corner house, as she planned to move her sisters and boyfriend Phil in with her, but, of course, Sara and I chose to buy houses next door to one another. We even took down the garden fence separating our two houses so we had a big communal space.

Feeling that it would be a terrible waste not to use the garages that came with our new houses, we also treated ourselves to a Mini Mayfair each. Sara's was black and mine silver, with lovely sky-blue velour seats. We loved our new cars, despite the fact they were tiny, and somewhat impractical, especially when I started dating Dave, who was six feet four. The poor bloke had to stick his head out of the sun roof. Down the line, when we were recording at PWL in Borough, Sara and I always took it in turns to drive, and on the way back home, late at night when the streets were empty, we'd put on the twelve-inch version of 'No More Tears (Enough Is Enough)' and see if we could make it home before the track, which was eleven minutes and forty-five seconds long, finished.

Having a garden meant I could get a dog. Chutney came from Battersea Dogs Home and was the first of several dogs I've owned over the years. After Chutney sadly died, not long after my son Tom was born, Sara and I got brother and sister Labradors, Paddy and Ruby, and shortly afterwards my little terrier, Rita, arrived on the scene. I bought Rita on a trip to Harrods when I was meant to be looking for soft furnishings. Typically, I got waylaid in the pet department and there she was, all alone in a cage. Of course, I couldn't bear to leave without her.

Sara and I spent hours on Hampstead Heath with Paddy and Ruby rampaging around, chasing sticks and swimming, with poor little Rita always trying to keep up with the big lads.

—

SARA: The moment the dogs arrived at the Heath, the yellow Labs would make a beeline for the nearest muddy puddle, fully submerging themselves like a couple of hippos with just their little brown eyes visible, refusing to get out. Back home, they'd dig up all the plants in our enormous communal garden; in fact, very little was safe from them. One lunchtime, I left a Sunday roast in the oven to cook, while we all had a quick drink at our local. My boyfriend and I returned to find Paddy had somehow removed the chicken and roast potatoes and devoured the lot.

During that whole era in the mid-eighties, our row of houses was quite the little community. Our friends Spud and Sue lived across the street, and we spent many a happy hour in The Malden Arms, which was run by Ken and Elaine and frequented by a little white poodle called Charlie.

Most Sunday evenings, Keren and I would take it in turns to cook. My speciality was moules marinière served alongside tequila cocktails. There'd be the two of us and our boyfriends Terry and Dave, and sometimes Spud and Sue. Keren's boyfriend Dave was mad about jazz, so Miles Davis was always on the record player, offering a soundtrack to some good red wine and debates about anything and everything. Sometimes Dave would play his trumpet in an attempt to infuse the evening with his own brand of jazz, though as the evening progressed, he often ended up ditching the jazz and headbanging to Led Zeppelin, occasionally using poor Chutney as a guitar.

Then one night in the autumn of 1984, we received a fateful phone call. Bob Geldof called Hillary to say, 'Get the girls down to the studio. I'm putting a charity record together.'

That was about all we knew about the venture when we agreed to do it. He and Midge Ure from Ultravox were planning to raise money in reaction to television reports of the terrible famine in Ethiopia, and the song was to be recorded all in one day at Sarm Studios in West London. The collective name for the assembled supergroup was to be Band Aid, and the song was 'Do They Know It's Christmas?'

The recording took place on a Sunday morning and after a Saturday night out we turned up bleary-eyed in Hills' Volkswagen Golf, only to see Sting walking towards us. Once inside the studio, we spotted the Duran Duran boys, happily mingling with their pop rivals, Spandau Ballet. Clearly, this was something big.

Before long, Sarm Studios was full of the great and good of the British pop scene: Paul Young, Phil Collins, The Boomtown Rats, Heaven 17, Culture Club and U2. The atmosphere was, of course, loud and boisterous, so Siobhan, Keren and I made our way over to Paul Weller. Paul, like us, was a bit more low-key than some of the other assembled pop stars, so the perfect person for us to hang out with.

During the recording of the big choruses, we were divided into two groups, and, being female, our higher

voices were able to cut through – although it was a close call with Bono's bellows. My main memories of the recording were Status Quo being great fun, and hearing George Michael sing live for the first time. He was standing directly behind me in the line-up, in his black and white checked shirt, and I couldn't believe how incredible his voice was.

—

KEREN: Bob was a real force of nature, putting the whole project together, and I'm still incredibly proud that we were part of it. Nobody in the studio that day realised the impact it would have, immediately and in the future. It drew the world's attention to the problem in a way that a news broadcast couldn't. That said, I'm mortified when I look back at the video now. There I am, with a fag and a coffee, looking dreadful. Who on earth would record vocals with a cigarette these days?

What's interesting, looking back, is that it was almost exclusively male artists in attendance; there were hardly any women. Just us and Jody Watley from Shalamar – that was it! Of all the pop artists there were in Britain, there were no female lead lines on the record.

8

'WHAT'S THE MOST EXCITING THING IN NEW YORK RIGHT NOW?'

SARA: It was in 1986 that we heard a song on the radio that would change our musical direction once again. 'You Spin Me Round (Like a Record)' by Dead or Alive was a hi-energy extravaganza, and we loved it. We had to find out who was responsible for this slice of pop genius – immediately!

The producers in question turned out to be a little-known production team called Stock, Aitken and Waterman, and we tracked them down to their studio in Borough. As huge as they became, defining the sound of British pop in the mid to late 1980s, hardly anyone had heard of them at that stage.

While at the studio, Pete Waterman played us a track they'd produced called 'Say I'm Your Number One' by Princess, of which we were big fans. They had also started working with a new young duo called Mel

Us and ALL the drinks, BRIT Awards.

and Kim – the Appleby sisters. Our first suggestion for collaboration was to record a cover of 'Venus', giving it their hi-energy treatment. They said it wouldn't work; in fact, nobody was keen on the idea, including our record company, London Records. The three of us were adamant that it would, so we persevered, and thank goodness we did!

—

KEREN: We worked on the now-famous 'Venus' dance routine with our friend Vaughn Toulouse. He came up with the iconic 'fire-arms' move, which audiences all over the world still join in with whenever we perform the song. 'Venus' was the first video where everything we'd set out to achieve was realised. In Peter Kerr, we found a director who really understood who Bananarama were, and what we were about. While the video depicted us as strong women, women who were in charge, it was all done with humour and with more than a little tongue in cheek – which summed the three of us up perfectly. We enlisted the help of a brilliant theatrical costume designer to complement our styling and bring our more ambitious ideas to fruition. We had met choreographer Bruno Tonioli a few years before when we made the video for 'Robert De Niro's Waiting, and he was back on board again, staging some incredible set pieces and bagging himself a starring role in a Gene Kelly pastiche. The recipe certainly worked, as 'Venus' shot to number one all over the world, including the US.

During this new and exciting period for the band, I discovered I was pregnant. This was a bit of a shock, but then again, maybe I should have seen the signs. Like when I'd insisted that the strap around my waist attached to the enormous headdress I wore in the 'Venus' video was making my stomach bulge. I only made a doctor's appointment because I felt a bit run down and didn't feel like going out partying, which wasn't at all normal. I was sick on the morning of the appointment but still didn't twig. Sara came with me in the car to South Kensington, which is where the doctor's surgery was.

'You don't *feel* pregnant,' the doctor said on feeling my stomach. 'But maybe we'll do a test anyway.'

133

'Right.'

When it came back positive, I was stunned. How could this be? My periods had stopped about six months before, so I'd come off the pill, which didn't suit me anyway. I'd started using the doctor's recommended form of contraception, the 'honey cap', which was supposed to be reliable (although several friends using it at the same time would dispute that).

Armed with this slightly bewildering news, Sara and I got back into the car in shocked silence. We drove aimlessly around for a while, finally parking outside Harrods where we bought a couple of big slabs of millionaire's shortbread from the Arco Bar, which was a favourite place of ours in those days. There, I cried, and I panicked. Sara was hugely supportive, and by the time we'd finished the shortbread and driven off, I was feeling much better. Still, I wasn't sure how my boyfriend Dave was going to react. He was, after all, only twenty-two, and we'd only recently got back together after a short separation. It wasn't perhaps the most stable of situations. As it turned out, he was thrilled and spent much of the next few months celebrating his virility. Some of the people from the label didn't take the news of my impending motherhood quite as enthusiastically. Some were concerned that it 'wasn't a convenient time', and that I was 'still really young'. There was even the suggestion that maybe I shouldn't have this baby, and should wait for the right moment. This wasn't what I wanted or needed to hear.

Instead we rejigged some of our upcoming plans. By

then, 'Venus' had gone to number one in the US, which was fantastic, and we were due to play some promotional gigs. We replaced these with a radio, press and TV tour, which involved lots of travelling, smiling, talking and having dinner with competition winners. I was now six months pregnant and throwing up after almost every meal. Even without the live performances, the tour was full-on and I became ill and exhausted. There are so many photos from that period with Sara and Siobhan looking radiant and beautiful, next to me looking bloated and knackered.

—

SARA: Before we set off on our US promotional tour, Pete Waterman threw us a massive party at PWL Studios to celebrate our Stateside success. We were all on a high, and the party turned into a fabulous night of dancing. It was almost beyond our wildest dreams that we were about to embark on a tour of America to promote a number one record on the US Billboard charts.

We'd recently taken on American management in the form of Ron Weisner and Bennett Freed. Ron had managed Paul McCartney, Madonna and Michael Jackson, so we were in good company. I have a fond memory of the three of us knocking on Ron's hotel door and Siobhan doing her best impression of Cilla Black's TV catchphrase 'Surprise surprise!' when he answered it. We just fell about laughing and he must have thought we were mad.

Travelling around all the different states, in our DMs

Interview at KROQ radio station, LA.

and BOY regalia, was both eye-opening and fun, and we were fortunate to experience it in the way that we did. On the west coast, Bennett and our tour manager, Topps, took us on a helicopter trip to Alcatraz Island in San Francisco Bay – the maximum-security prison where Al Capone had once languished. It felt incredibly glamorous, soaring across the bay to the island, but on the way, it became apparent that Bennett had come equipped with a bag of toys from a local joke shop. During the tour of Alcatraz, he let off a whoopee cushion during the black-out moment of what should have been a terrifying 'solitary confinement' experience. He also left fake dog excrement outside the cells, just to watch the reactions of the other tourists. So, despite the glamour of the helicopter ride, it quickly descended into pure juvenility.

Later that night, we had dinner in a beautiful little town called Sausalito. The views of San Francisco were spectacular, with all the lights twinkling in the hills.

While in Minneapolis, we were invited to Prince's nightclub, First Avenue. At one point during the evening, we were standing with Prince, watching the action from the VIP area above the dance floor, when the DJ played 'Venus'. It was such a trip watching everyone rush forward, swamping the dance floor. It was at times like all these I realised how lucky I was.

—

KEREN: After the promotional tour, Sara and I stayed on for a holiday in New York, flying our boyfriends out to join us. It felt wonderful spending some extra time there; we often don't get to experience the cities we're working in, and the Big Apple was a favourite for both of us. Plus, I was in dire need of a bit of R&R by then. We booked rooms at the legendary Gramercy Park Hotel; Humphrey Bogart married his first wife there, and JFK once lived there for several months. Other notable guests included Debbie Harry, The Clash and David Bowie. We loved the bohemian vibe of the place and, while we were there, we allowed ourselves to be total tourists, even taking the train to Coney Island.

During our stay, there was a grand four-day celebration for Liberty Weekend – an extra-special one, as it was the centenary of the Statue of Liberty. Ronald Reagan gave a

Heatwave in Coney Island.

speech, accompanied by the French president, François Mitterrand. After the formalities, we were invited to join a party on the MTV boat on the River Hudson, along with thousands of other boats. It was a spectacular sight, culminating with the mother of all firework displays. ZZ Top were performing, and a host of stars joined us, including Andy Warhol, who we'd previously met at the MTV Awards in New York, and who seemed as thrilled to see us again as we were to see him. He spent much of his time hanging around taking Polaroids of us. He'd recently been asked by the *NME* what was the biggest thing happening in New York right now, and had answered, 'Bananarama!' I nearly fell over when I read it.

It was an exceptional day and, despite not feeling my

best, I was completely carried away by the atmosphere and excitement, knowing it was an experience I was very unlikely to repeat in my lifetime. I refused to accept that pregnancy should change or inhibit me, aside, of course, from not drinking or smoking. In fact, I continued to go out as much as I could, although I'm not convinced Sara's attitude was especially helpful. As sympathetic and supportive as she'd been when I found out I was pregnant, her mantra now was: 'You're only pregnant, for God's sake, you're not ill!' She was always full of handy tips and advice too, such as 'Just throw up and come out!' Her attitude certainly shifted when she was pregnant a few years later, when she refused to travel after six months – no early mornings, late nights and traipsing around America during a heatwave for her.

Before Tom was born, we had to prepare for the release of our next single, 'Trick of the Night'. As part of the promo, the record company arranged for us to be part of a BBC TV show called *In at the Deep End*. It was a programme in which the presenters Chris Serle and Paul Heiney undertook various tasks as complete beginners in professional roles. In this instance, it was making a pop video. I was very heavily pregnant by now, but, as was generally the case, nobody made allowances, and a night shoot was arranged. By the early hours, I was utterly exhausted, which resulted in me having a complete meltdown in the mobile home that was our dressing room, crying hysterically. Hills had to talk me round, but eventually, red-eyed and puffy-faced, I finished the shoot.

Unfortunately, the resulting video wasn't at all what we had in mind, so in the end, we had to shoot another one. This one was a lot easier for me, as I was only filmed from the neck up while sitting in a chair. Bliss.

Meanwhile, I became a very convenient taxi service for nights out. I couldn't drink, so why not take the car? That way, I could ferry Sara, Terry and Dave back and forth to wherever we were going. After a night out at Heaven, under the arches at Charing Cross, we arrived back at my house in Kentish Town to find that someone had parked across my drive so that I couldn't put the car away. To a tired, pregnant woman, this was a massive deal. It seemed that my neighbour was having a party, and his guests were parked randomly around the street. 'Don't worry, we'll sort it,' Sara said, and she and Terry headed off to knock on the neighbour's front door, which was eventually answered by a man in a red latex catsuit and holding a cat o' nine tails. It really shouldn't have been a surprise. My neighbour, who on the surface was a very sweet pensioner with grey hair and a beard, had previously warned me this kind of thing might happen.

'I'm turning my garage into a torture chamber, dear,' he'd said, like it was the most natural thing in the world. 'So, if you hear a lot of banging from next door, don't worry, it'll most probably be that.'

If he hadn't told me, I'd have guessed anyway, as I was forever getting leaflets about S&M services through my letterbox.

—

SARA: Once inside our neighbour's house, we found ourselves in the kitchen having an interesting conversation with a butch lorry driver in a long blond wig, a twin set and pearls, while beyond him various people lay strewn across the floor in outlandish positions. All this to a soundtrack of goth music that seeped through the townhouse. Our neighbour asked if we'd care to see what he'd turned his bedroom into. Even though we'd really just come in to find out whose car was blocking the drive, curiosity, of course, got the better of us. We made our way upstairs, following the creaking and yelping sounds, and arrived in his bedroom to discover a rack of sorts. To be honest, it was more IKEA – if IKEA had made racks – than it was heavy-duty S&M.

Nevertheless, one eager party-goer was happily strapped to it. I had to laugh as my boyfriend turned to me muttering, 'Oh, for f—k's sake,' in his strong Belfast accent. Still, there was no harm done and, in the end, the car was moved.

—

KEREN: A few days before my due date, which was New Year's Eve, my consultant told me my blood pressure was up. The doctor also remarked that I hadn't grown much and that the baby felt small. An appointment was made for me to be induced at the Portland Hospital on 29 December. I wasn't sure if this was necessary, or because the doctor had plans for New Year's Eve and just didn't fancy being called in.

Once in hospital and induced, I waited patiently, but nothing happened. They tried again, and when labour eventually started, it was like nothing I'd ever felt before. I waited for the promised gaps between contractions, but there didn't seem to be any. I'd always thought I had a high pain threshold, but this was so intense, any ideas I'd had about natural childbirth went quickly out the window. Instead, I screamed for the anaesthetist, who was busy with another patient. In the meantime, I had gas and air, which did nothing apart from making me somewhat abusive, especially to Dave, who I blamed entirely for getting me into this mess.

Eventually, the anaesthetist came to administer an epidural. It was a bit troublesome, as there wasn't much respite between contractions, but when it finally kicked in, it was bliss, and I fell asleep in front of the TV. A little while later, the monitor indicated that my baby was in distress, so I was rushed out of my lovely birthing room to an operating theatre. As it turned out, I didn't need a caesarean, and Tom was born at 5.40 a.m. the next day. He was eight pounds and one ounce, so clearly not as tiny as the doctor had led me to believe.

I've spoken to some friends who seemed to find childbirth quite an enjoyable experience. Still, I was adamant that I was never doing it again. I hated both the pregnancy and the birth, and I felt bloody dreadful afterwards. I spent at least forty-eight hours vomiting into what looked like a grey cardboard top hat. On the New Year's Eve of 1986, Sara, Terry, Dave, Mel, Vaughn, Phil Dirtbox (our friend who ran the warehouse club nights called Dirtbox) and, for some reason, Fat Tony, arrived to toast the newcomer with champagne. I was hardly in the mood for a celebration of any kind. Still clutching my cardboard top hat, I couldn't wait to see the back of them. Before I left the hospital, I was encouraged, nay forced, to have some photos done. They weren't the most glamorous shots I'd ever had taken, but they still ended up in all the tabloids.

I had a room full of flowers and well-wishers galore, but I wasn't bothered. Tom was the only thing I cared about. He was beautiful. Perfect. Now I just had to learn what I was supposed to do with him.

9

GIRLS JUST WANNA HAVE FUN

KEREN: Mercifully, Tom was a good baby, and I loved spending time with him. When he was about eight months old, we moved to a much bigger house on the other side of Kentish Town. The new place boasted high ceilings, huge windows and lovely period features, and I stayed there right up until I moved to Cornwall. Sara and I were no longer neighbours, but we still saw each other most days. Phil Dirtbox lived in the next street with his Texan girlfriend Eugenie, who Sara and I adored. Towering

over six feet, she was a real Southern belle who modelled for Jean-Paul Gaultier among others. At this point, our soirées seemed to become a little more diverse. Phil was really good mates with Keith Allen, who always kept us entertained and was a frequent visitor along with ballet star Michael Clark, or Mickey C as we liked to call him.

—

SARA: We'd met Keith Allen a couple of times at the Groucho Club, and I remember him coming to pick Keren and me up once in his car. It was a somewhat strange experience, as he'd turned the front passenger seat around to face the back. His explanation for this was that it meant he could easily hold a conversation with whoever occupied it. We headed to the Cobden Working Men's Club in Notting Hill for some kind of party, which was brought to an abrupt end by the partial collapse of the ceiling.

Michael Clark was known as 'the enfant terrible' of contemporary dance. We knew a dancer in his company, Les Child, who we'd met through our friend Baillie Walsh and who went on to choreograph our video 'Only Your Love', and we would watch them perform at Sadler's Wells. One of the most memorable times being the avant-garde ballet, *I am Curious, Orange* in 1988, which felt more like a gig or a party and featured music by The Fall. Occasionally a performance would include Leigh Bowery who, considering his immense stature, was extremely agile.

By then, my boyfriend Terry and I were living in Abercorn Place, St John's Wood, just around the corner from Abbey Road Studios. Terry was particularly happy with the location, being a huge fan of The Beatles, particularly John Lennon. I'm not sure how but at one point we had a four-track recorder in our house which the Beatles had used back in the sixties. It was duly returned but perhaps inspired the amazing version of The Beatles' song 'Rain' that Terry's group, The Adventures, performed when they supported Fleetwood Mac at Wembley Arena.

—

KEREN: I guess I hadn't really thought about how hard juggling work and motherhood might be. I just imagined I'd get on with it as I always did. As much as I loved being Tom's mum, the workload involved in being in Bananarama was full-on and it was clear that I

needed help, so our old friend, Mel, became my part-time nanny. I was young and didn't want to miss out on the life I'd had before Tom was born. Some evenings, I'd read him stories and sing to him, as my dad had done to me. I must admit, my repertoire was quite limited and somewhat repetitive. 'I Will Always Love You' (the Dolly Parton version) or a bit of Crystal Gayle usually kicked things off, and sometimes I sang Bananarama songs. Once he was asleep, I'd sometimes go clubbing, arriving home in the early hours, but I always, always made sure I was up a few hours later to have breakfast with him.

Feeling slightly guilty that I'd had to slow down and take time off at what was pretty much the peak of our career thus far, I felt as though I needed to get back to work as quickly as possible after Tom was born.

We'd already started the *WOW!* album and, after the success of 'Venus', there was a feeling that it was going to be huge. I agreed. *WOW!*, I felt, was the perfect style of music for Bananarama. Pure, slick, pop!

—

SARA: Stock, Aitken and Waterman were typically a self-contained writing and production team, but we already had a track record of self-penned hits under our belts, so they were happy to co-write with us. Mike Stock was the keyboard player of the trio and a great songwriter. He was the main guy when it came to putting the basic backing tracks together, with the help of Matt Aitken. Pete Waterman was a huge music fan and knew all the club records from New York, Italy and the UK. He was also well versed in who all the great songwriters and producers were; a real font of knowledge. He'd walk into the studio while we were working and throw in an idea before disappearing off, while Siobhan, Keren and I worked on the top-line melody and lyrics with Mike and Matt. After the success of 'Venus', helped along by Peter Kerr's brilliant video and Vaughn's choreography, we wrote 'I Heard a Rumour'.

For this video, we enlisted choreographer Bruno Tonioli. He had previously worked on the 'Robert De Niro' video, which had no choreography, so I guess he'd been there for the staging of the different scenes. He brought his then-boyfriend Paul Cavalier on board, as well as their friend Baillie Walsh. We rehearsed at Pineapple Dance Centre in Covent Garden, which, in the eighties, was like stepping into a scene from the Alan Parker movie, *Fame*. On the first day of rehearsals, Paul and Baillie arrived in their shorts, all ready to be fabulous. Keren and I took one look at Paul, with his bleached quiff and flushed face.

'We're not dancing with him,' we said in unison. 'He looks like a poodle.'

The boys were models, not dancers, so for them, Bruno's routine was quite taxing. It was hilarious rehearsing together, with the boys carefully counting out loud, and over the coming weeks, we all became great friends – as we are to this day.

'I Heard a Rumour' was a huge hit and went to number four in the US. We travelled around the UK performing it on the wealth of music shows that existed in the 1980s, and it was probably one of the happiest periods of my life.

Baillie and Sara throwing some shapes on the dance floor.

Spending so much time with the boys meant we had to find ways to amuse ourselves, which wasn't exactly hard with three hysterically bitchy queens along for the ride. We all loved letting off steam after a TV appearance, and on one occasion we were invited as guests of honour to a plush new club in Newcastle. The supply of all-night free drinks was never going to be the best idea. That particular night started serenely enough, but as the evening went on, things got wilder and wilder until, at one point, Paul

149

Seaside Special in Jersey (top); Montreux Music Festival.

ripped my Jean-Paul Gaultier skirt. I, in turn, ripped his
Ralph Lauren jumper, and before I knew it, Baillie was
swinging me around in the air on his shoulders. He ended

up with huge scratch marks down his back, which was unfortunate, as he had to cancel a swimwear shoot he'd booked for the next day.

—

KEREN: Amid all the fun nights out, there was still much work to be done. To hone our dancing skills, Bruno encouraged us to take classes with him or his assistant at Pineapple. I can only remember laughing at our attempts to jeté across the studio, sounding more like a herd of elephants than ballet dancers. We even attempted a few tap classes, but the teacher was quite impatient and made Siobhan cry. Bruno's instruction for moves was always the same: 'Butch, butch, butch and butch . . . and then link it together with a step, darling.'

We had such a riot in the dance studio, and the influences for our moves came from the most unexpected sources. The first move in the dance for 'Love in the First Degree', for instance, was a direct steal from Les Dawson doing the *'Blankety Blank* chequebook and pen'!

We made many foreign trips with Bruno and frequently visited his flat in London where he cooked delicious Italian food. His recipes usually involved a 'sowse', which was 'sauce' in Bruno speak, and after dinner, we'd all play cards. Our favourite game was called Sevens, and it was a regular feature of Saturday nights with Sara, Bruno, Paul, Baillie, hilarious friends Tony Martin and Babs von Vag, and me. I'm not sure if Bruno ever realised how much we all cheated, passing cards under the table, so he was always left with the pack when the idea was to get rid of all your

Filming the 'I Can't Help It' video in LA with Bruno
(top); Bruno's kitchen.

cards. He also had a microphone at his flat, which he'd
plug into the stereo for karaoke nights.

On one trip to LA with Bruno, we stayed at the Sunset
Marquis, which was our favourite hotel there. The hotel

Jessica Rabbit eat your heart out. Fashion designer Roland Mouret's creation for *Movin' On*.

Rehearsals for the 1989 World Tour, Pineapple Dance Studios *(above)*.
You Give Love a Bad Name, somewhere in America *(below)*.

Backstage with one of our loveliest long-standing fans, Takuro, Tokyo *(top left). Every sha-la-la-la, Every wo-o-wo-o, still shines,* karaoke, Tokyo *(top right). Rockin' the Gaultier fishnet, German TV (above left). If you like Pina Coladas...* with Jax and Bassey Walker *(above right).* Home of the legends *(below).*

The Three Musketeers, 1988 *(above)*. All the glamour by Ellen Von Unwerth, 1991 *(below)*.

Twist of Lemon? *I Can't Help It* video, LA *(above)*. Having the worst time ever! *(below)*

Fun and games in Florence with Baillie, Jeffrey Hinton, Tallulah, Big Sue and John Maybury *(top left)*. Pre-drinks at Keren's with Michael Clark, Eugenie, Jacquie O, Dave Scott-Evans and Phil Dirtbox *(top right)*. I Love You, Rio *(above left)*. At the wedding of The Cure's bass player, Simon Gallup *(above right)*. Just the two of us *(left)*.

Could we have a little more fun please? With June and George *(above)*. Gotcha!, Rio *(right)*. Quiet night in at Sara's *(below)*.

Pure bliss hedonists, St Tropez *(above)*. Cowboys and Angels with George and Roger Taylor from Queen *(below)*.

Dinner at George's house in Goring *(above)*. Daphne's in Chelsea *(below)*.

Ultra Violet, 1995, styled by our good friend David Thomas.

Who would have thought a shoot in a car park could be so glamorous...

Nights out with David Thomas and Oliver Hicks *(above left and right)*.
It's cold in New York *(below left)*... But hot in Marbella *(below right)*.

Christmas in Cornwall with Andrew,
David Thomas and Keith Flint *(above)*.
Ibiza nights, Pikes Hotel *(right)*.
Here come the girls: Sara with Pepsi
and Shirlie, Necker Island *(below)*.

Alice, Keith and his pot-bellied pigs, Great Dunmow, Essex *(above)*.
Sara's birthday with the lovely Keith Flint, Soho House *(below left)*.
The start of a beautiful friendship, Tokyo, 1994 *(below right)*.

With Simon Halfon *(above left)*... on his target rug in LA *(above right)*. Thanks for the lift! Sara and Keren with Noel Gallagher, Meg Matthews and Paolo Hewitt *(below left)*. Oops *(below right)*.

It's Mugler darling! Video shoot for *Only Your Love*, 1991.

is situated in West Hollywood and is well known for its clientele from the music business and movie industry. Sara and I were staying in one of the hotel's apartments along with Sara's boyfriend, while Bruno and Hills were in rooms at the main hotel. At one point, while I was in the huge walk-in shower room, Sara popped her head in to see if I wanted breakfast. She disappeared briefly, then came rushing back in, looking slightly concerned.

'The bacon is on fire,' she said.

I thought she was exaggerating, but she wasn't. By the time I got out to the kitchen area, flames were licking the ceiling, and the room was filling up with thick black smoke. We both went into a panic, not knowing what to do. We would probably have been stupid enough to throw water on it had Sara's boyfriend not leapt out of the bath and soaked a towel, which he then threw over the blaze. What was even more embarrassing was when we glanced out of the window, only to see all the other hotel guests lining the streets outside. Clearly, a fire alarm had been triggered by Sara's burning breakfast, and the Sunset Marquis had been evacuated. Bruno has since re-told this story, insisting he was making a Bolognese 'sowse' for us when the fire started. Not so! In fact, I'm not even sure it's possible for Bolognese to catch fire. It was Sara's bacon that did it. It wasn't the first time we'd had issues of this kind either. In Chicago with Pete Waterman, we'd accidentally set off the hotel fire alarm after a night out and, once again, the whole hotel had to be evacuated.

—

SARA: On another occasion, sometime in 1988, Baillie called me up and asked if I fancied going with him to Italy for a few days. His then-partner, filmmaker and artist John Maybury, was putting together the production for a runway show – I think it was for the then relatively unknown fashion designers, Dolce and Gabbana. I headed to Florence with Keren and a fabulous mix of Baillie's friends. Sue Tilley, or 'Big Sue', was an incredible wit, and a friend of Leigh Bowery's, working as a promoter and cashier at his club, Taboo. Through Leigh, she later met the artist Lucien Freud, and sat for a series of paintings for him, while she was a supervisor at a Charing Cross benefit centre. The resulting works are now worth a fortune. In 2015, one of them, *Benefits Supervisor Resting*, sold for £35.8 million. In Florence, Sue's primary job was to toll the bell at the end of the catwalk to signify the show was about to commence. Baillie also brought along Space and Jeffrey Hinton, who were both DJs, and a six-foot-six bleached blonde called Tallulah, who was the gentlest, sweetest man you could hope to meet. Tallulah had a penchant for nipping off to buy pizza all the time, even after we'd just eaten. We'd often catch him in various doorways, en route somewhere, stuffing his face. Bananarama were at the height of their fame, so we tended to cause quite a stir wherever we went, especially with such an eclectic bunch of people in tow. It was a bit like a circus troupe coming to town. After Florence, we headed to Rome on the night train for more fun and games.

Baillie had a flat on Charing Cross Road, a prime spot next to the National Portrait Gallery. I don't know what the deal was, but the rent was cheap and apparently he could stay there for ever. The flat was on the third floor, and the living room contained only a vast wooden throne and a giant glitter ball. Each week, Keren and I would arrive at his flat for pre-drinks before our pilgrimage to a club night called The Daisy Chain, at The Fridge in Brixton. At the flat we'd meet up with John Maybury, Leigh Bowery, who was a little afraid of us after we accidentally hit him on the head with a spinning yoyo, his wife Nicola Bateman, and fashion designers Rifat Ozbek and Stephen Linard. Other regulars were Michael and Gerlinde Costiff, and the late Alan McDonald. We called him 'Furniture Alan' because he made furniture at the time, but he went on to become an award-winning production designer on *The Queen* and many other movies. Last, but not least, was stylist and creative director, Jerry Stafford.

—

KEREN: Sara and I loved nights out at The Daisy Chain at The Fridge in Brixton and the theme nights were a particular favourite. I once found myself empty-handed en route to 'Handbag Night', so stopped our cab to grab a large police sign with a handle on the top of it, before continuing our journey across the river.

Jeffrey Hinton was the club's brilliant DJ, spinning a real mixed bag of music, but always filling the dance floor. We only knew the lights were about to come on when he played Joan Jett's 'I Hate Myself for Loving You', the last song every week, and then it was a race

155

outside to grab a taxi for what seemed like the endless journey back to north London. It was often quite a raucous affair, and I rarely came away without some sort of bruise or scrape from the enthusiastic dancing. Of course, we were bound to become friends with Jeffrey. He shared a flat with ex-Blitz kid, DJ Julia, later to be known as Princess Julia, in Camden. If Sara and I weren't hanging out at Baillie's in Charing Cross Road, we were often to be found there.

—

SARA: Another favourite haunt was Café de Paris, a very opulent venue with chandeliers and a wrap-around top floor overlooking the dance floor with winding stair-cases either side of a stage. It first opened in 1924 and luminaries such as Marlene Dietrich, Josephine Baker and Judy Garland had all performed there. Keren and I were there most weeks, and at one point it became the venue for one of the most eclectic and influential club nights of the era: Kinky Gerlinky, run by Michael and Gerlinde Costiff, with whom we'd become good friends through Baillie. It was a place where clubbing culture met outrageous fashion. There was regular live music, drag performances and catwalk shows. One evening after a catch-up over drinks at the Groucho with our lawyer and friend Chris Organ, we decided to treat him to the Kinky Gerlinky experience. As we led him down the stairs, into this world of wonder, he was uncertain if this was the place for him. However, once he had a drink in hand, he seemed to settle in, although he didn't stray far from the bar or from us. After a while, Chris called it a night and Keren and I descended the staircase into the flamboyant disco ball below.

—

KEREN: During the nineties, Soho became less sleazy and more of a Mecca for the gay community, bringing a different but equally exciting vibe. Just a short hop from Baillie's Charing Cross Road flat, there was a multitude of bars and restaurants, like Balans, to choose from before heading off to G-A-Y at the Astoria, which became a regular haunt for Sara and me as both clubbers and performers. I was really sad when Crossrail and gentrification put paid to the Astoria. By the time we were recording *WOW!*, we'd embraced Soho and the gay scene wholeheartedly. In fact, Sara and I became such regulars at Heaven, ever since the club night there, Cha Cha's, in the early eighties, that if it was busy at the bar – as it invariably was – we had the manager's permission to help ourselves to drinks. Sometimes, on boys-only nights, Sara and I would be the only girls in the club's cavernous entirety.

We'd also pop into Madame Jojo's on Brewer Street to watch the drag shows, where, on one occasion, we were faced with a hilarious version of ourselves. A drag Bananarama! I might well have been insulted, what with drag-Keren being a short, fat queen who, at one point, burst into tears and ran off the stage, but I wasn't.

It was a time when life felt good to me. I had a beautiful young son, and I was enjoying work and all the success and joy it brought. Sands were shifting, however. I could hardly have imagined when we started recording *WOW!*, just how much things would have changed by the time we finished it.

Tower Records, LA.

10
END OF AN ERA

SARA: I'm not sure exactly when Siobhan starting seeing Dave Stewart from Eurythmics. For a while, she kept it to herself, so we had no clue there was a relationship happening. In 1986, while we were doing some filming at MTV in New York, Keren and I went to Siobhan's hotel room to ask if she wanted to come out with us. Her door was wide open, but she was nowhere to be found. On further investigation, we noticed that wherever it was she had gone, she had applied some false eyelashes so it had to be be a date.

The following day there was a photo of Dave on the wall at MTV. I think that was when she told us they were seeing each another.

When we'd started work on the album *WOW!* with Stock, Aitken and Waterman, we all loved what was coming out of the writing and recording sessions, but at some point in 1987, things started to go awry. It was obviously a culmination of many factors but I do remember there was a heated debate between Siobhan,

Mike Stock and Pete Waterman about Dave Stewart winning the Best Producer award at the 1987 BRITs, which he'd also won the previous year. Having pretty much dominated the charts that year I think Mike and Pete felt they deserved the prize, and the atmosphere in the studio, and subsequently the recording of the album, seemed to deteriorate from there. At the time, we had no idea if Siobhan had plans to leave the group but what we did know was that her life was changing dramatically. She was pregnant and preparing to get married, and spending much of her time in LA with Dave.

—

KEREN: As time went on, we saw less and less of Siobhan. It felt like she'd lost interest in the band and the album, and the tensions between us were palpable. As Siobhan herself has often said about that time, 'The rot had set in!'

It's difficult to know if Dave's influence was a part of her decision to leave the band, but I think it's fair to say he was no big fan of Stock, Aitken and Waterman. I think Siobhan was looking for a way out, a change, and Dave was offering the means of flight. She busied herself preparing for her wedding in France, and after they were married, she moved to LA permanently. With our album unfinished, Sara and I continued recording the remaining vocals on a couple of tracks without her.

As Siobhan was getting close to having her baby, we flew to LA to film our next video, with no idea that it would be our last with her. The song was 'I Can't Help It', and I'll give Siobhan her due, she was a hell of a lot more enthusiastic and animated than I'd been when pregnant during the 'Trick of the Night' video. That said, she did decline to do the final scene, which entailed us all splashing around in a milk bath with a bunch of butch men. It was probably just as well, as the whole thing descended into a free-for-all and full-on fruit fight.

For the duration of the shoot, we stayed at Siobhan and Dave's house in the valley, with Sara and I sharing a room. It was all very lovely until the night we awoke to violent rumbling and shaking, with no idea what was happening. When we jumped out of bed to find the bedroom floor shaking, we realised it was an earthquake. From the window, we could see the water sloshing out of the pool. It was pretty scary and seemed to go on for ever.

I'm not sure if we knew it was the end when we left LA to come home, but we certainly had more than an inkling that Siobhan would be leaving the group way before we were told it as fact.

—

SARA: A few days before the BRITs, Hills told us Siobhan was leaving the band. We'd been on such a roll with the hits: 'Venus', 'I Heard a Rumour', 'Love in the First Degree'; we were flying high. It just felt like at the height of our success, she'd disconnected from her past and vanished from our lives. While there was a certain sense of relief from both sides, there was also a sadness at the end of an era and, for now at least, the end of our friendship.

There's a big difference in what I felt at the time and what I feel in retrospect. It's obvious that people grow and change and want to move in different directions, but at the time we had been living in each other's pockets for so long that it felt monumental. There's been a lot of emotional processing over the years, and whilst I don't see Siobhan that often, when we do get together it feels just like old times.

—

KEREN: We'd been in limbo and, while it was a shock, now we knew at least we could move forward. That night at the BRITs was the occasion when, despite all our years of success, we received our one and only nomination, for Best Video for 'Love in the First Degree'. British pop was such a boys' club back then and male stars were always having scantily dressed women dancing in the background for no apparent reason, so we decided to reverse the trend with our BRITs performance that evening. There were a few dissenters in the ranks when we asked the dancers to don black skimpy underpants and black over the knee socks – essentially stockings – for the performance, but they all succumbed to our wishes in the end.

We had a fabulous final blast performing 'Love in the First Degree'. We'd had six-and-a-half years together, the three of us, and that was something to be celebrated.

And given how it felt like we were still fighting for respect and recognition in the industry in 1988, it was great to see us and our swathes of hot male dancers featured so prominently on the recent BRITs retrospective. I guess it was quite an eye-opening performance for the time, as the reaction of the audience and the show's host, Noel Edmonds, attests.

Since that night and over the years, we've all talked, laughed and disagreed about what happened during that time. It won't come as a surprise to hear that Siobhan views certain events differently, but as (almost) fully fledged adults, we're finally able to discuss it calmly, and even to air our grievances.

11
WYOMING TO WEMBLEY

SARA: After Siobhan's departure, we bounced back with renewed energy. Our record company was keen to keep the visual dynamic of a trio, but since our group had been built on friendship rather than anything manufactured, we knew we couldn't audition session singers. Jacquie O'Sullivan was someone we remembered from the early eighties club scene who'd been in a band before. Despite not knowing her that well, she seemed like a great choice and she replaced Siobhan in February 1988.

Jacquie turned out to be a breath of fresh air: chilled and funny, with a great voice. The first thing she did was replace Siobhan's vocals on our next single, 'I Want You Back'. We shot the video and, a few weeks later, we were back on *Top of the Pops* with a Top Five hit. 'Love, Truth and Honesty' followed in September of that year, then a greatest hits album in October, which achieved triple-platinum sales, and then another single, 'Nathan Jones', in November. That single became our eighteenth chart hit, and we entered the *Guinness Book of World Records* for being the world's most charted female group.

Finally, it was time to tour, and a world tour at that. We'd rehearsed in preparation to tour on a couple of occasions in the past, but that had been off our own bat. With the advent of MTV, the record company didn't really think touring was necessary, realising it was easier to send pop artists off on promo tours armed with their latest videos rather than the costly alternative of putting them on the road. That said, London Records were a great company to be signed to. It always felt like a family, and I felt very supported by everyone there,

With Mariella at her house in the Cotswolds.

particularly Roger Ames, Pete Tong, Eugene Manzi, Julia Marcus, Tracey Bennet and his then girlfriend Mariella Frostrup, who was our PR for seven years.

We remained friends with Mariella long after working with her. Down the line, we spent time at her and Tracey's beautiful cottage in Eastleach in the Cotswolds. When I was pregnant, my partner and I stayed there. One evening he brought some logs in for the fire, and tried to split one with an axe, but instead shattered the glass top of a gorgeous French coffee table. We were both mortified.

Keren and I often went clubbing with Mariella, and enjoyed several rather 'highbrow' parties with her, making the acquaintance of the journalist and political broadcaster Andrew Neil, who nicknamed me Olga, because of my white-blond hair, which I wore in two 'space buns'. Andrew was hilarious fun, full of wit and charm. He invited us to a summer party at his house in London, where guests included political journalist and TV and radio presenter Robin Day and future Prime Minister, Tony Blair. At one point in the proceedings, Mariella and I were having a perfectly lovely time, enjoying drinks on the terrace, when we heard a commotion coming from inside the house. It turned out to be Keren, berating chef Delia Smith for trying to jump the queue for the bathroom.

When I look back now at the gargantuan task Jacquie had – learning the back catalogue of songs and all the dance routines, before embarking on a short series of live dates in Japan followed by a world tour in which she was totally thrust into the limelight – I take my hat off to her. She was truly amazing. Aside from being a good singer, Jacquie was funny and easy-going, but she also had the same mad, mischievous sense of fun that Keren and I had.

The Love Kids Tour of 1988 was a sort of warm-up for the upcoming world tour, with three sell-out concerts at the Budokan in Tokyo, a venue that The Beatles had played two decades before, plus shows in Osaka and Nagoya. It was awe-inspiring arriving at these large venues to see people queuing around the block. For the shows, Keren and I had asked our friend John Maybury to put together some footage. He'd shot some black and white film of us at his house, which was played in slow motion on giant video screens behind us. It looked amazing. It was such a thrill experiencing Japan all over again, this time with Jacquie. We also took Baillie along for the ride. He was interested in filmmaking, so came to capture life on the road: temples in Kyoto, the fashion, food, mad-as-hell Japanese TV appearances, and, of course, the concerts themselves. There were moments of uncontrollable laughter in some of the TV interviews, with Baillie sniggering behind his camera, barely able to keep the lens focused.

Back in London, Hills received a phone call from Dawn French and Jennifer Saunders. They'd filmed a spoof sketch about us for their TV show, with Jennifer playing me, Dawn playing Keren and Kathy Burke playing Jacquie, and sent it over for us to view. In it they were interviewed by Paula Yates as they attempted to record a track in the studio. They then enlisted the help of Kevin

Godley (from the group 10cc and now a video director) to 'make the video', for which the only requirements were that they had white faces and red lips. Dawn's quote was, 'I know it can be done, I don't know if you can do it', a phrase Keren and I love and use all the time. Being a comedy sketch, it wasn't flattering but it was hilarious. We got on really well with all three of them and are still in touch with the Cornish goddess Dawn.

A while later, we had a meeting at the BBC with Dawn and Jennifer, where they invited us to perform on Comic Relief with them. We chose the Beatles track 'Help!' and the six of us recorded it at the PWL studios, which was great fun. We quickly choreographed the accompanying video, which featured our dancers plus French and Saunders regulars, Raw Sex, fag-smoking and topless. The performance on Comic Relief was epic, with tables of cream pies all ready for us to throw at each other at the end of the song. If you watch closely, you can see us all getting ready for the onslaught on Dawn.

Then rehearsals for our first world tour began in earnest. This time no one was pregnant and it was really happening. It was a huge deal and would see us on the road for three months. It was then when we met the wonderful Steve Levitt, who put the whole production together. Bananarama had never toured on this scale before, so we put our complete faith in him and his team, leaving everything in his hands. It worked out well and Keren and I still use Steve today; we adore him.

As with everything we ever did, we were hands-on. Putting together a tour band was not something we had experience in, but we ventured down to John Henry's rehearsal studios in Brewery Road, King's Cross, for the auditions. There we sat through the lengthy process of listening to numerous guitar riffs, drum solos, bass lines and electric keys. It was exhausting. Several days later, with auditions complete, we took the advice of our newly appointed MD, Dave Ital, and chose the young, talented and super-enthusiastic musicians for the tour.

—

KEREN: We threw ourselves into dance rehearsals at Pineapple in Covent Garden. It had become a second home to us in the eighties, and I still got a kick out of watching all the 'proper' dancers through the blinds. You'd have thought that dancers would treat their bodies like temples, but in those days, the communal areas were filled with smoke. I asked some of the dancers why they all smoked, and the stock answer was that it helped keep the weight off. We had amazing dancers – two brothers, Bassey and Norman Walker, and Paul Swaby – who brought a completely different vibe to the new show. They added energy and funkiness to the dance routines. They certainly had their own interpretation of some of our camper moves, which made for a completely new dynamic. The whole vibe was, dare I say it, sexier! Although not to the point we wore heels. God forbid! We simply teamed our chunky brothel creepers or shoes by Patrick Cox (or Pat the Cobbler, as he was known to us) with various fabulous outfits.

We knew designer David Holah from the gay scene.

John Derrybunce and David Holah, at the Astoria.

He and Stevie Stewart had founded a clothing label called BodyMap. We chose our favourite pieces from their collection, embellished them, and then had some other stuff designed. We started rehearsals with four costume changes, but one of them, which involved a mini-tutu, had to be canned, as we just couldn't get in and out of them in the allotted time.

The band were superb and, after rehearsing in the usual dump of a rehearsal room, we got to strut our stuff on the full production stage.

—

SARA: On the sound stage, we were able to bring the entire production to life. The size of this operation was massive; like nothing Bananarama had ever done before. Now the tour was an impending reality, complete with a full band and what seemed like a hundred crew members.

Our first dates were in Boston, so we kicked off with two weeks of rehearsals there. During some downtime, Keren and I met up with my Uncle Lee and his family. He was a professor at Harvard, and we wanted to have a look around the famous institution so he took us for dinner at one of the very swish restaurants on its huge campus. It was wonderful visiting his and my late Auntie Mavis's family home, which I remembered seeing in photographs as a child. Back then, I'd been fascinated by what looked like lollipops sticking out of the grass all along the long drive leading to the house. They turned out to be light reflectors.

On the first night of the tour, we did some filming with MTV in our dressing rooms and then we made our way to the stage. Typically for an opening night, disaster struck, and there was a technical hitch. We had to spend a full ten minutes chatting nervously to the audience while technicians worked to fix the problem.

Apart from that, once we were up and running, it was a huge success. Just like so many other things with Bananarama, performing with a full live band on massive stages was something we learned to do as it was happening.

Our opening look for the tour had a Spanish flavour. White satin ruffle-sleeved blouses with strategically placed sequin studs to catch the light; high-waisted, black, stretch pencil skirts with a kick out ruffle at the back with large, black fedoras; black tights and the Patrick Cox shoes. The backdrop to the set was painted with enormous, swirling 1960s patterns and flowers. The stage was two-tiered with steps that the dancers had to navigate in the dark before the spotlights hit us at the start of the show on our arrival through the floor of the main stage. The opening number was 'Nathan Jones', which was choreographed to within an inch of its life and executed perfectly. However, as the dancers' entry onto the stage was in darkness, on one occasion Norman took a tumble down the stairs. Luckily, he had the skill and agility to hit his first position just as the lights hit him. It was truly a remarkable feat.

For some of the longer trips between dates, we flew across America, but what we really wanted was to experience 'life on the road' with the full-on tour bus just like we'd seen on TV and in the movies. It made for long journeys, but I wouldn't have missed it for the world. The camaraderie between us, the band, the dancers and crew was like nothing I've ever experienced. It was like a huge family. Most of our team had just finished a tour with Prince, so they really were at the top of their game. It was clear that they really loved us, and we felt the same. So much so, that if ever we were invited out for dinner, we'd insist that they all came too. Keren and I had also invited our friend Mel along as wardrobe mistress, as well as DJ Jeffrey as her assistant.

We'd drive for hours across the Midwest through

mountains and deserts: one minute hailstorms, the next blazing sun, and always the long highways you see in the movies. In Wyoming, we stopped to eat at a truck stop in the middle of nowhere. The scene reminded me of the film *Bus Stop* with Marilyn Monroe. It looked like it was frozen in time, with mini-jukeboxes on the tables playing fifties music. The waitresses were all in their forties or fifties with beehive hairdos, huge earrings, blue eyeshadow and pink lipstick. They looked brilliant if a bit freaky, but I'm sure they thought the same about us, with our ripped jeans and backcombed hair.

—

KEREN: The bus had a dedicated area at the back with a neon 'PARTY' sign. This was where we congregated after shows when driving overnight to the next venue. Here we danced, partied, sang songs accompanied by guitars, played cards and watched movies. The bus also had these coffin-like claustrophobic bunks upstairs, which were barely big enough for one, although they frequently contained two. How rock 'n' roll!

I ended up celebrating my birthday in Salt Lake City, although not necessarily in my usual style, as it was pretty much alcohol-free. The real party was postponed until the next night in Denver.

Before each show, we played music in the dressing room, having a bit of a dance and singalong to get us warmed up and in the mood. We had a boom box on which we played cassettes; Mel had a mixtape which included 'If I Had A Hammer', which wouldn't have been my first choice, but ended up becoming a firm pre-show favourite, complete with accompanying dance routine. Kate Bush's greatest hits and The Smiths were also a must for warming up the voice.

—

SARA: After a fantastic show at the Universal amphitheatre in LA, I think we had two weeks off. In retrospect, I'm not sure how that was financially viable, with everyone still on the payroll. It certainly wouldn't happen now! But hey, what did we know or indeed care? We were in our twenties! We were staying at The Sunset Marquis again, which really was our go-to place. Aside from almost burning it down, it was here we'd met Mike Tyson a few years earlier, who sat on the front of his limousine singing 'Cruel Summer' as we came towards him on our way back from breakfast at Mel's diner on Sunset Boulevard. At the time, I couldn't believe he'd recognised us, but even more unbelievable was the size of his neck. We once got chatting to the singer Rick James, who invited us to an LA warehouse party, where we danced all night before thumbing a lift home at dawn. About eight of us ended up jumping into the back of a pick-up truck, hair blowing in the wind, with not a care in the world.

—

KEREN: We spent most of our time at The Sunset Marquis around the pool, and sometimes went for a quick dip after hours, which was strictly forbidden. If ever a member of staff appeared, we'd jump out, dripping wet, and play innocent.

'Have you been using the pool, madam?'

'No, of course not!'

This was a fairly common occurrence given our penchant for nocturnal visits to hotel pools in various exotic places. And while it's not advisable to swim after the partaking of alcoholic beverages, I was on hand to administer the old 'hand under the chin' rescue technique I'd learned as a child, when the need arose to drag one of our dancers to the safety of the steps one night.

Aside from the dodgy blokes on the French disco tour, we'd never had any kind of security before. Simon Cook, who we'd met with his twin brother, Viv, when they were doing security for Duran Duran, looked after us on this, our first world tour. He had an unenviable task, trying to corral all three of us. It must have been like herding kittens. On nights out, he'd get one of us out of a club, and while he was going back for the others, the one already outside would slip back inside. Sometimes, he'd propel me into the back of a taxi, only to watch me climb out the other side. That said, Jacquie and Mel could out-party all the rest of us put together. There was one occasion when we had to get the hotel staff to open Jacquie's room up with a master key, and drag her out of bed for a soundcheck. As for how Mel and Jeffrey managed to get the costumes washed and ironed between shows, well, that's a complete mystery. I imagine plenty of hand-washing in hotel baths and hairdryers was involved.

—

SARA: From LA, we headed to Australia for the next leg of the tour, staying at the Sebel Townhouse in Sydney. Australia was a blast, and some of the gigs were quite different from the ones we'd played in America. One night, we played at a rave where the lovely Stefan Dennis, Paul Robinson from *Neighbours*, came backstage and then joined us for a few days on the tour bus.

—

KEREN: On the Japanese leg of the tour, I was overjoyed at the prospect of being with Tom. By this point I had a full-time, live-in nanny, Jo, who accompanied him on the flight, and on the days leading up to their arrival, I could hardly wait to see him. As soon as they got to the hotel, I ran straight to Jo's room for what was a joyous reunion. He was only two at the time, so regular phone conversations simply couldn't make up for the chance to experience a big squeeze from his tiny arms. During our first show in Tokyo, he came careering down the aisle shouting, 'Mummy!' and waving frantically, closely followed by a red-faced Jo in hot pursuit. But in addition to the shows there was a lot of promotion in Japan and I didn't get to spend as much time with Tom as I'd have liked before we had to move on to the next country, and Tom and Jo had to fly back to London.

We did three shows in Manila, the first of which was very strange. The section of the audience we could see from the stage didn't seem to be reacting at all. It was only when the rest of the audience were illuminated that we saw people going crazy. Apparently, the local dignitaries had bagged all the best seats.

Backstage, the band, and particularly the dancers, were beside themselves when American martial artist and actor Chuck Norris, who was filming there, came to say hello and hang out. In Jakarta, we had the strange task of running the entire show at soundcheck in front of a censorship panel, so they could make sure we weren't too raunchy. We toned it down for them and passed muster; then we did the show the usual way.

My abiding memory of the Asian leg of the tour was that it was absolutely boiling. In fact, it got so bad we had to have oxygen shipped in for our costume changes after Jacquie passed out with the heat. In Bangkok, the air conditioning broke down, so it was completely unbearable. The dancers generally came off stage looking drenched, but that night we all looked like we'd just done the ice bucket challenge. As we headed to our dressing rooms, someone informed us that the Queen of Thailand would like to meet us.

'Sorry, that's great, but we need to shower first before we meet any queens,' I said.

After a quick spruce-up, Sara and I decided to have a little lie-down but must have dozed off – which is something I usually find impossible after a show because of the adrenaline. Hills, meanwhile, was banging on the door, getting understandably anxious at the amount of time we were taking, but on that occasion, there was no shifting us. Eventually, when we resurfaced, I had to navigate the disaster of my bright red face and panda eyes before I was photo-ready for royalty. Astoundingly, the Queen of Thailand and her children had patiently waited and were thrilled to meet us and us them.

From Bangkok, we went to Whitley Bay, which is quite an extreme change in surroundings by anyone's standards. It was great to be back in Blighty, though. When you're travelling to so many places over that length of time, you can lose all sense of reality, with no concept of what's been going on at home – especially back then, pre-world wide web!

—

SARA: The UK was the last leg of the tour and heralded a big moment for us: finally playing Wembley Arena. It was such a thrill, and something Keren and I couldn't even have dreamed of back when we were recording songs on cassettes in our bedrooms. The whole thing had been an extraordinary experience, and looking back I feel sad that we didn't get anyone to film one of the shows. It seems incredibly remiss given it was such a massive tour at the height of our fame. We do have our own home movies of it, which Jeffrey filmed, including our backstage warm-ups to Kate Bush. I have very fond memories of the boys moonwalking and body-popping to The Smiths. I'll have to dust off the

VHS tapes and locate a VHS player from somewhere – if they still exist – just to relive it all again.

—

KEREN: We threw a big end-of-tour party to celebrate our success. George and Andrew from Wham! were there and particularly complimentary about the show. We hadn't really spent much time together before. Little did we know how that would change in the very near future.

12

SUN, SEA AND ST TROPEZ

KEREN: I first met George Michael on a blind date. It was a feature for *No.1* magazine, the glossy, weekly pop mag that rivalled Smash Hits throughout the eighties. George was very late for the date, which was something we later came to expect, probably because he was blow-drying his hair. I'd grilled the journalist about who was coming beforehand, hoping for John Taylor from Duran Duran. Even after the journalist gave in and revealed that my date was to be a member of Wham!, I was hoping for Andrew. Anyway, it was George, and while the so-called date wasn't all that memorable, the resulting picture in the magazine was horrendous; both of us with big fat faces, looming up from the page.

Of course, we knew both George and Andrew a little throughout their Wham! career, but we really started socialising with George after Wham! broke up. We had a good mutual friend in Simon Halfon, who did the artwork for George's record sleeves.

George was the most incredibly generous person,

both with the charities he supported and with his friends, but not necessarily with the free Harrods notepaper. Games nights were a big thing for us back then and, it may have been only once, but he chided us for using more of his complimentary Harrods notepaper than was strictly necessary. I imagine the comment was much regretted when Simon did our bidding and brought it up in front of Elton John.

At games night, we'd play Beat the Intro and Celebrity, the game where you pull names out of a bowl and describe a famous person. George hated losing as much as Sara and I did. He'd always try to split us up because we often had a one-word code or a facial expression for a fair few of the celebs we'd loaded into the bowl.

'It's not fair!' George would say, several times throughout the evening.

We also loved what we called the Rizla game, also known as 'who am I'. George wasn't out publicly at the time, but we all knew he was gay so it was a running joke that we would stick the name of someone outlandish and camp on George's forehead. At some point he would invariably end up asking, 'Am I a camp old queen?' and we'd all say, 'Yes! but back to the game!' We never tired of that one.

—

SARA: George used to send his driver, Dennis, to pick us up from my house before driving us back to 'Weeping Ash', which is what George's home in Hampstead was called – much to our amusement. Once there, Dennis would get out of the car and ring the bell and, over the intercom, we would hear the strains of George's hairdryer going full blast. He was never ready! George loved a party, and back in the day, he threw the best ones. They were often lavishly catered, and our love of caviar meant we made a beeline for the kitchen where the buffet was beautifully laid out. We didn't bother building dainty blinis with all the trimmings, we just scooped it onto our plates. After enjoying the buffet, we'd dance the night away, along with our favourite regular guests: Pat 'the cobbler' Cox and Tim 'Timbo' Jefferies. Sometimes, we'd chance upon the likes of Sir Ian McKellen or Richard and Judy relaxing by the pool in George's gorgeous garden. Whatever happened and however long the party lasted, Keren and I would always reconvene at the buffet at the end of the party to scoff any remaining caviar.

—

KEREN: For George's thirtieth, he arranged a coach to take us to Newmarket races where we were given vouchers to bet on the horses from the comfort of a giant marquee. I think I lost all my money on the first two races.

Betting on the gee-gees was just the preamble to the main event – a seventies-themed party in another marquee, this time at his father's stud farm in Hertfordshire. Once we arrived and changed into our fancy-dress costumes, the festivities continued, with a full-on disco plus a covers band who found themselves with plenty of guest singers among the partygoers.

The guests at George's parties were generally people he felt comfortable with, so he always seemed relaxed and was able to be himself. Mind you, it wasn't always this way. We went on a fair few overseas trips with him, and occasionally, in public, he became George Michael, the star! Once, heading out of Heathrow, he strode over to check-in, with Sara and me in tow.

'Leave this to me,' he said, approaching the woman at the British Airways desk.

'Hello, I've been told to make myself known to a member of the BA staff,' he said.

'Why?' the woman said. 'Who are you?'

Of course, we fell about laughing, and George was fuming.

'God, that had to happen in front of you two, didn't it?' he said.

At Nice Airport, Sara asked him to give her a hand with her suitcase when it came off the luggage carousel.

'I can't be seen carrying that! I'm George Michael!' he said.

We always told him exactly what we thought, and I like to think he found our honesty refreshing, although he did once say, 'Thank God I've got a big ego, or you two would destroy me!'

That's probably why George invited Sara and me pretty much everywhere, except to meet Elton John. When we asked why we weren't allowed to meet Elton, George told us that his ego couldn't take it, with our endless jokes at his expense.

Once we discovered the joys of good restaurants,

there was no looking back. Sara and I preferred busy, buzzy eateries rather than some of the more subdued fine-dining restaurants where the atmosphere was so quiet it was like eating in a library. Langan's was a favourite in the eighties, and a place where we knew the menu without looking at it. We always started with the delicious soufflé aux epinards, with sauce anchois. We also loved The Ivy, where there's always the option of comfort food like shepherd's pie. It seems quite ridiculous now that back in the 1980s, restaurants were full of smokers, who'd puff away alongside all the non-smokers, leaving them stinking like an old ashtray.

Dining out with George Michael took things to another level, and was always a no-expense-spared experience with the best tables and the finest wine. We often went to Le Caprice in St James's and when Quaglino's first opened up, I made the most spectacular entrance, falling from the top to the bottom of the magnificent metal central staircase. I made such a clatter with my heels, while desperately clutching at the rail, that every diner in the massive, hangar-like space went silent, turning around to look. Of course, I tried to mask my pain and embarrassment as I hobbled to our table in full view of the amused diners.

—

SARA: One night we went for dinner at Crockfords Casino in Mayfair, with a couple of friends, and played some after-dinner blackjack. George gave everyone a little cash to gamble with, and we all got lucky. So lucky, in fact, that our friend, Kate, bought a new kitchen with the proceeds.

With our winnings, George suggested that Keren and I accompany him to Paris for the weekend and stay at the Ritz. The hotel, of course, was stunning, and our rooms were gorgeous. George was an excellent host as always; each night he'd take us for dinner at some lovely restaurant and we'd all end up dancing the night away at Le Queen before heading back to the Ritz with an entourage in tow.

On one trip to the south of France, George drove us all from the airport, through the gorgeous French countryside. We had the roof down, and I remember us singing 'One' by U2 at the top of our voices. Other times he'd arrange for a helicopter to pick us up and deposit us in the garden of his villa. Keren and I were very impressed. On arrival there would be a rapid change of clothes before we went off to dine at the Hotel Byblos, with its renowned in-house club, Les Caves du Roy. A combination of jeroboams of champagne and fireworks meant these nights invariably got very raucous.

—

KEREN: For a few years, Sara, George, his friend David and I went to St Tropez regularly. On the first trip, we stayed in a lovely boutique hotel – Villa Bastide de Belieu, I think – and then with George at his villa in the hills just outside of the town. Afternoons lazing by the pool were idyllic. Sara had a video camera, and one afternoon when George had popped inside to do some work, we started filming one another: swishing around the pool, waving our sarongs around with the James Bond theme blasting out in the sunshine. Of course, George couldn't resist the limelight, so rushed outside to join in with the fun. It would have been the perfect memory to have captured, but later when we tried to watch it back, the footage had disappeared. George must have sneaked into Sara's room and erased it all. Admittedly, there had been a split second in the proceedings where he had revealed a little more of himself than he might have liked, but we were furious to find that he'd deleted the whole tape.

St Tropez was always fascinating. We all spent many an evening eating dinner or sipping drinks at the quayside restaurants, marvelling at the people who seemed happy to dine on their flash yachts while hordes of tourists on the promenade stood gawping at them. Aside from the blatant displays of wealth, there was usually a fair amount of diabolical plastic surgery to behold as well.

—

SARA: The one big mistake George made was giving Keren and me the entry code for his house in Highgate. As I only lived five minutes away, the two of us would often let ourselves in, unannounced, if we were bored, just to see the dogs or ask if he fancied having lunch – which he always did. Unfortunately, we weren't so adept at getting out of the house with the keypad. On one occasion, as the sun was coming up after an all-night party, we couldn't fathom how to get the gate to open from the inside, and a couple of stragglers behind us couldn't manage it either. In the end, we had to make a distinctly inelegant and cumbersome escape, which involved getting a leg up onto a wall and hauling ourselves over a spiked gate. Remarkably, there were no lasting injuries.

The fun times Keren and I had with George are almost too many to mention, from walking our Labradors in the Cotswolds to being flown to Brazil for Rock in Rio. Rio was followed by a week's holiday in a gorgeous resort called Buzios where one afternoon George demonstrated his distinct lack of skill on the football pitch.

There was a lot of evening entertainment, including professional dancers who, after finishing their performance, asked if anyone would like a quick lesson in the lambada. George and my boyfriend jumped up eagerly for a go but were actually dreadful. The song of that holiday for me and my boyfriend was 'Kiss From a Rose' by Seal. I remember playing it while sitting on the rocks near our apartment staring out to sea.

Another time, George chartered a private plane to take twenty of his friends on a two-week holiday to Richard Branson's Necker Island. My boyfriend at the time, Bassey – one of the dancers from our world tour – had the unenviable choice of coming on the holiday to Necker Island or dancing with Michael Jackson. MJ was his childhood hero, and the job was dancing in a video

Michael was shooting in Germany. In the end, he chose the job. Keren was also unable to come as she and Andrew Ridgeley had already committed to doing a *Hello!* magazine spread in Tuscany. I was left flying solo. The only other guests I really knew were the very lovely Martin and Shirley Kemp, but I got on well with George's new Brazilian boyfriend, Anselmo, and his sister Mel. The beautiful hideaway in the British Virgin Islands was an absolute vision on arrival. This was pure luxury and I felt really privileged to be there. Each room had a stunning view of the crystalline blue water and golden sand. Every meal was a feast. Each morning we would all meet at the long breakfast table in the warm early-morning sun. George had booked the island exclusively so we had the playground to ourselves and it felt like an incredibly decadent school trip. We lazed around sunbathing all day, drinking cocktails, having barbecues on the beach and disco dancing all night.

One afternoon we set off on a scuba-diving trip but, having never done it before, I was slightly apprehensive about falling backwards off the boat with a weighty tank of oxygen on my back. Once aboard we started trying on our wetsuits and one by one lined up for the departing fall into the water. We were instructed to hold a long rubber line as we swam out ready for the dive. Martin was great and dived first time, followed by the other guests, but after a few attempts I was too scared to take the oxygen mask out of my mouth, which was part of the safety test, and bobbed back up to the surface. On coming up I was happy to see that George was also bobbing on the surface after a few failed attempts, but he persevered and finally did it. It really was such a wonderful holiday and a very happy time.

The last time I saw George was, as it turned out, ten months before he died. Andrew Ridgeley was cooking dinner at George's house in Highgate, and they invited me over. The three of us reminisced and laughed, and George was adamant that we all play Scrabble before we leave. Writing this reminds me of what an amazing, kind, generous, funny and talented friend he was and how much fun we packed into our lives. He is missed and will always be in my heart.

13

POP LIFE

KEREN: After the dreamlike state I'd lived in during the fantasy world of the tour, I came down to earth with a bit of a bump. I was, of course, thrilled to be back at home with Tom, but after all the highs, facing the reality of everyday life wasn't easy. It was like the biggest dose of post-holiday blues you could ever imagine. The bright spot on the horizon was that we had a brand-new album to write and record.

—

SARA: My songwriting had come a long way from 'What a Shambles' on *Deep Sea Skiving*. Having started with the indie style of 'Aie a Mwana', then learned from the invaluable experiences of writing with Jolley and Swain, and the brilliant uber-pop of *WOW!* with Stock Aitken and Waterman, I was ready for something completely different. We'd met Youth years before, in our early clubbing days. Now, he was a fast-rising record producer, and we were thrilled to be working on tracks with him for our new album, *Pop Life*.

I've always enjoyed songwriting, but I think on this album, I was pretty prolific. This was in no small part due to Youth's music, which greatly inspired me. The backing tracks were brilliant. When Keren and I first went to his studio, which was at his dad's house in south London, he played us tracks he'd been working on. Some of them were quite basic, others we started from scratch, and a couple were more fully formed with a chorus or a verse. I remember 'Tripping on Your Love', for instance, already had a chorus, so I wrote verses for it.

Each song sounded different, and there was a wealth of technology at our fingertips, which made experimentation easy and all the more fun. Unlike the fast pace of PWL, Youth gave us as much time as we needed to play around with ideas and fully immerse ourselves in the process. We experimented with drum loops and new, state-of-the-art sounds with Youth's attitude being 'try whatever you want, anything goes'. It was very refreshing.

This album was really important to me. It was Bananarama mark two and a very different direction to the records we'd made with Siobhan. Jacquie wasn't involved in the writing of *Pop Life*; I guess because we just continued with the set-up that we'd been used to. As she explained in an interview around that time, 'I think it's really hard for three people to write together when you're writing about things close to you.' I agree; I've always preferred writing lyrics on my own. Who knows, though, what might have happened if we'd made a second album together?

I worked really hard on this album, writing most of the lyrics and a few melodies. Youth would throw in title ideas like 'What colour are the skies where you live?' and 'Only Your Love', and along with Andy Caine, a singer/ songwriter, who Youth had introduced us to, Keren and I would work on other melodies. Andy was pretty awesome, both vocally and as a person. We had a memorable night out watching Luther Vandross at Wembley, when, at the end of the night, we tried leaving through a back route but ended up climbing over a high security fence. Andy got entangled at the top of it, and unable to move for laughter, instructed us to go on without him.

Andy was a real asset in the studio, coming up with great vocal ideas, and I really enjoyed recording with Jacquie. Her voice really enhanced our sound. Keren and I have always loved arranging harmonies and instrumentation, but Youth's production helped take it to another level.

We hadn't lost our sense of the ridiculous either. Whenever there was a break in the proceedings, Keren would take to the piano, hammering out abstract chords while Jacquie and I performed expressive, contemporary dance. One night, Keren and I burst into an impromptu rendition of 'Underneath the Arches' with a full dance routine. This was an ancient song we both remembered from watching *The Good Old Days*, a TV show in the 1970s. It left us all in tears of laughter.

—

KEREN: *Pop Life* was a real shift in direction for us. I listened to it recently, and today, as I write this, it's the thirtieth anniversary of the album's release. I loved the freshness and creativity of working with Youth and Andy, although the writing sessions, which were at Youth's place in far-away Wandsworth, were a pain in the arse to get to. If I'm honest, had I been in a better place, mentally, I might have contributed more to the writing of *Pop Life* than I did. The truth was, this was the start of a very tough period for me, but I have great memories of working on the melodies and harmonies with Sara and Andy, and it's an album of which I'm hugely proud. When I listen now to songs like 'Preacher Man' and 'Only Your Love', I feel we hit new highs both musically and in our subsequent performances. Maybe it was having a successful world tour under our belts, but we just seemed to exude confidence during that period.

The promotion for the album was also great fun. We enlisted the help of our old friend Paul Cook to play the drums, and it felt great to have him back in the fold. Having met both him and Youth at the age of eighteen,

it sort of felt like we'd come full circle, but ended up in a different place . . . if that makes sense.

Style-wise, this was one of my favourite periods too. The album cover shoot we did with the iconic Ellen von Unwerth is, in my opinion, the best we've ever done. I still have the Gaultier fishnet top and the leather chaps we wore, just in case I ever need them for fancy dress, like the red Antony Price dress which I wore in the 'Movin' On' video, which was perfect for my outing as Jessica Rabbit.

In the summer of 1991, sometime after our last single from *Pop Life*, 'Tripping on Your Love', Jacquie and I sat down to have a chat. By this time, the three of us had toured, made an album, shot videos and appeared on TV all over the world, but somehow, Jacquie was still seen as the new girl. This didn't seem like something that was going to change any time soon, and I think we all felt it.

Sara and I had too much respect for Jacquie just to have her there, making up the numbers while we made all the decisions. In the end, we all agreed that we should go our separate ways. We'd crammed a whole lot into those few years and had a whale of a time, but from here on in, Bananarama were going to forge ahead as a dynamic duo.

—

SARA: Our emergence as a duo seemed to coincide with a shift in the musical landscape. At the age of twenty-six I'd come across an article that said, among other things, that Bananarama were pushing thirty and should, therefore, call it a day. It came as a shock that women, in particular, should have a shelf life or shut up shop just because they were over twenty-five. Fortunately, this wasn't a universal opinion – we had some loyal supporters in the media, as well as our fans – but there were a fair few slights of this kind to endure. A well-known male journalist and ubiquitous talking head summed up our early career with the observation that Bananarama were 'just a hairstyle'.

By the early nineties, the big 3-0 was indeed looming, and, like Keren, I was about to become a mother. We were hardly ready for our free bus passes, but the thinking from some areas of the music industry seemed to be that we were somehow outstaying our welcome. I, however, refused to be defined by a chart position, my date of birth, or the decade we were currently in.

Over the years, some of our harshest critics have been women, who often seemed jealous or dismissive. It was baffling. We'd always steered our careers, written our own songs, made our own decisions. We were passionate, decisive and driven. We weren't manufactured or moulded by record and management companies, but still, we weren't given any credit. When you're young and trying to find your identity in the glare of the public eye, it can make you terribly self-conscious. Whilst there were plenty of supportive and complimentary comments and reviews its the occasional bad ones you remember. Attacks and backhanded compliments by men and women, suggesting we were nothing more than our red lipstick and backcombed hair, became tedious and were just plain rude. While we shrugged it off and carried on, it was, at times, demoralising. When talking recently about some of the negative media coverage she'd had, including her fashion sense, Michelle Obama said, 'It leaves a mark on your soul.' That really resonated with me.

I remember being shocked when we found out that Janet Street-Porter had booked us on a TV music show she was producing, presuming she might have the same negative opinion of Bananarama. Janet was quite the opposite, telling us that she embraced our spirit and our strength, which made me feel good. At that age, it was something I needed to hear. We were, after all, only in our twenties.

By contrast, the female presenter was very condescending. 'You've never played live – can you sing?' she asked.

I wondered if she'd have asked male artists the same question.

'Have you ever thought about writing your own material?' another (male) journalist asked midway through an interview. We were two albums into our career by then, and had co-written most of the tracks. I went from buoyant to deflated in about two seconds.

Another time, singer/songwriter Billy Bragg rallied various pop stars to voice their opinions regarding the 1984 miners' strike. We weren't feeling hugely prepared, but as we were discussing what we wanted to say ahead of being thrust in front of the cameras, a female celebrity loudly remarked, 'I know, why don't you say, "You can't be in a pop group unless you're thin and pretty?"' The room was full of testosterone and with that bitchy comment, our confidence was further undermined. We were furious.

On the face of it, these slights may seem very trivial. To me, though, they are not. They are a significant reflection of how females are perceived, portrayed, and treated in society.

I often found it hard, as I think we all did, not to become defensive or to counter-attack in these situations. We were women with differing opinions who wanted a say in our career and our music. Some people found that hard to accept. It was easier for them to dismiss us, to label us difficult and obstructive or fluffy and unimportant.

—

KEREN: The trouble is, it is very easy to hold onto the negative comments and forget all the positive ones. When we were younger, we expended so much energy trying to convince everyone that we took our music as seriously as our male contemporaries. It was exhausting. In the end, I thought, God, I just want to enjoy our achievements. I needed to let go of any resentment I had against people whose opinion didn't matter to me in the first place.

I know what I am, and I don't really care what you think. It was very freeing to get to a point in my life where I could genuinely feel this. There is, however, still the odd comment that gets my back up. When we did our reunion tour in 2017, a female journalist wrote some particularly bitchy comments in her tabloid newspaper column. 'Get your zimmer frames out' was a cheap shot, particularly coming from a woman who was of a similar age to us. It's all too easy to become invisible as a woman in your fifties, and I would have expected a little empathy and solidarity. Maybe even a positive comment about how incredible it is to be still working in the industry and putting on a fantastic show on a hugely successful sell-out tour.

During some of our recent rounds of promotion, we've met some brilliant women who credited us with being their role models growing up. The fact that we became successful wearing Dr Martens, dungarees and donkey jackets and didn't conform to some male ideal or sexual stereotype is something I'm very proud of, and I like to think it's a positive example. As far as I'm concerned, it's OK for women to wear anything, or next to nothing if it's a personal choice. However, there is often still pressure on female artists to be sexy or skinny, and those attitudes can be harmful when they're passed on to the young girls who look up to their idols and feel they should look or act similarly.

—

SARA: The gender imbalance in men's favour is still alive and kicking in the music industry. Female artists, for instance, are still grossly under-represented at festivals, and in songwriting, production, publishing, and many other areas. Thankfully it is a problem that's being addressed, albeit slowly. While women continue the fight for recognition and representation, what we also need is for more men to understand and appreciate the problem and get involved. Personally I never saw any difference between the male bands and us when we started out and neither, quite frankly, did they. I loved working with Fun Boy Three, jumping on stage in Holland to perform with The Cure, and driving down to Bath to write songs and play Boggle with Tears for Fears. These bands weren't chauvinistic; they were inclusive.

That's not to say that we didn't experience sexism – we did, and that sexism took many forms: the over-familiar, long hugs from some radio DJs, the attempted groping in the back of a limo on a US promo tour, the lip service paid to us when we asked if we could put guitars on a track. It's a struggle at times and that's why I support and celebrate every female artist out there. Whether it's your time now, or your time is yet to come. Never give up and never give in. We belong on the stages of the world.

We've always tried to take things in our stride, tough

things out, and deal with it the best way we know how, by continuing to make music. We had each other too, which made it easier to bear. The more knock-backs we got, the stronger we became; and the more we learned about the music business, the more we stood our ground. Bananarama were not to be messed with! While it's true we have been surrounded predominantly by men in this business, I'm happy to say that the vast majority have been respectful and supportive. Occasionally these days, we encounter men who tell us how terrified of us they were back in the day, which seems ludicrous to me, and we all have a good laugh about it. Fortunately, most of the people we encountered understood and embraced us.

—

KEREN: There was one comment during that early nineties period that has never left me. We were trying to get a record on radio playlists at the time, which was all-important for the success of a single. The feedback from the programmers at a playlist meeting was that we were both mothers now, so no longer the right demographic for their listeners. So was that it? Suddenly, because you're a thirty-year-old woman with a child, you're done. Ancient. Not relevant any more. Your ability to make music has somehow evaporated? I was so appalled and upset by it, but it's what we were up against. Not for the first time, it felt like it was two of us against the world; and I guess it was after the world tour, and during the recording of *Pop Life*, that it all started taking its toll.

Photoshoot in Paris for the *Exotica* album, 2001.

No photos please *(above left)*. Never a dull moment *(above right)*. *Exotica* promo in Paris with ridiculous hair extensions *(left)*.

Drama album press shots, 2005.

Will it be our audience? Performing at the Singapore Grand Prix 2012 *(top)*. So proud to have performed at the 2012 Olympics in London, such a monumental occasion – we even had our nails painted! *(above left and right)*. On stage at Horse Guards Parade, Beach Volleyball final *(below)*.

Supporting and performing at the Breast Cancer Awareness event at the Royal Albert Hall *(top left)*. Appearing on *Watch What Happens Live*, Andy Cohen's TV Show, NYC *(top right)*. On tour with our band in the USA – we were told these were the best burgers in town! *(above left)*. Album signing at Borders bookshop in LA *(above right)*. Watching *The Eagles* perform in the desert, post sandstorm, Dubai with Marc Carey *(below left)*. Soundcheck at the opening of the Hard Rock Cafe in Dubai *(below right)*.

On set for our video *Look On the Floor*, directed by the late Tim Royce, 2005.

Viva album press shots, 2009.

Sara and her daughter Alice on holiday in Portugal *(above left)*. Alice with Keren's son Tom, climbing trees in Cornwall *(above right)*. Keren and Tom at Hampstead Heath taken by Tom's father, Dave Scott-Evans *(left)*.

Alice wearing Sara's vintage Dolce & Gabbana suit post photoshoot *(right)*. Bananarama win *Glamour*'s Icon Award – Alice, Tom and Keren at the afterparty, 2017 *(below left)*. My Mum is in Bananarama – Tom attending Beat Herder music festival *(below right)*.

Alice and Sara walking off their Christmas lunch, Gloucestershire *(top left)*. Sunset horse ride, Red Rock Canyon, Las Vegas *(top right)*. The daughter she never had – Keren and Alice Boxing Day drinks *(above left)*. The bambinos at Bruno Tonioli's BBQ *(above right)*. La Biennale di Venezia *(below left)*. Little Al *(below middle)*. Little Tom with Ruby and Rita, Kentish Town *(below right)*.

In Brighton with Ian Masterson and Dan Williams *(top left)*. At *Duck & Waffle* for Sara's birthday with Ian Heggs, Alice, Albert Samuel and Paul Cavalier *(top right)*. George Michael's summer garden party with Sir Ian McKellen and Patrick Cox *(above left)*. Breakfast in Positano – Keren with her brother Matthew *(above right)*. Besties at Booby's Bay, Cornwall *(below)*.

Behind the scenes for
Stella Magazine cover
shoot, 2017 *(above left)*.
With Peter Loraine at
*The Graham Norton
Show (above right)*. On
the famous red sofa
with Harrison Ford,
Ryan Gosling, Reese
Witherspoon and
Margot Robbie, *The
Graham Norton Show
(left)*. Performing *Robert
De Niro's Waiting* on
The Original Line Up
Tour, 2017 *(bottom)*.

Lights, camera, action! Bananarama 2020 *(top). An Evening with Bananarama* – hilarious fan Q&A *(above left). In Stereo* album cover, 2019 *(above right).* Performing at *An Evening with Bananarama* tour *(right).*

The overflowing Avalon tent – should have put us on a bigger stage! Glastonbury 2019 *(top left)*. A well-deserved after-show G&T, Glastonbury *(top right)*. Backstage and performing at BBC Radio 2 Live in Hyde Park, 2019 *(above, left and right)*. A rapturous Aussie welcome, The Enmore Theatre, Sydney, 2019 *(below, left and right)*.

Performing at the 20th Anniversary of Japan's Summer Sonic Festival, Tokyo and Osaka, 2019.

Our laughs are limitless.

14

SOMETHING'S GOT TO GIVE

KEREN: As a child, I didn't realise my mum was suffering from depression. As far as I was concerned, things seemed pretty idyllic really, despite the lack of cash. Every Saturday, we'd visit my Great Auntie Elsie and Great Uncle Ernie, who were unmarried, and lived in a village out in the country. On the way, we'd stop and get out of the car, so my brother and I could run in the woods, picking bluebells when they were in bloom. Elsie and Ernie were from a different generation and didn't have 'all the mod cons', as my mother would have said. When we got there, I'd run to the rainwater butt and dunk my head in, because I'd been told it would make my hair soft. There was no bathroom at the house; they still had an outhouse and a tin bath, which they put in front of the fire. They also had a cool, slate pantry, a forerunner to the fridge.

While we were there, my brother and I would play in the vast garden, which was always full of fruit and vegetables. In summer, we'd come home with hoards of strawberries and raspberries. On Saturdays, we picked carrots and greens to have the following day with the Sunday roast, which would be followed by a family affair at our grandparents' house, where we'd eat cake and play games like Creep Mouse and What's the Time, Mr Wolf? Our particular favourite was SUB, a game invented by my Uncle Joe, loosely based on wrestling. I would think of Uncle Joe when Tom and I invented silly games, like the James Bond game, where we played the Bond theme while Tom clutched the duvet and I whirled him around until he couldn't hold on any more.

Holidays back then were low-budget, West Country outings, usually wet, and involving the odd sandcastle and a camping gas stove in a cave to heat beans. Still, I always hated going back home and wanted desperately to live by the sea. Maybe it was seeing that same longing in Tom that later prompted my permanent move to Cornwall.

My dad and Sara's, Bob and Reg, were so similar. They never complained about anything and instilled strong values in us. My lovely dad, Bob, worked shifts in a factory and, as the buses only ran during the daytime, regularly walked the six miles to work, whistling as he went as if he was the luckiest man alive.

Mum was different. As the years went on, she either didn't want to or just couldn't face seeking help for her depression, however much I tried to persuade her. I suppose that was one of the many issues brushed under the carpet back then, that we're all much more aware of now. I was as guilty as anyone for dismissing her depression, pointing out to her that she had a home, family and lovely husband. What did she have to complain about? I didn't understand that depression is an illness. I suppose my perception was that Mum was being selfish and wallowing in self-pity.

When I first suffered from depression, I too brushed away my feelings of despondency. I didn't want to talk to anyone because I was embarrassed. My relationship with Tom's father, Dave, broke down not long after the world tour ended. For the first time, I had time alone with myself and discovered I didn't like me very much. I'd thought I could be everything to everyone, but now I felt I had failed on all counts. I cried lots, drank too much wine, and wallowed in self-pity, just as I imagined my mother had. It was like history repeating itself.

Now, I can see how the stress of trying to juggle motherhood and hold onto relationships while I was always travelling with the band took its toll. Ultimately, I knew I had to tackle my depression. I didn't want to end up with the mental issues Mum had suffered, because I couldn't stand the thought of it impacting Tom. Still, it was tough for me to open up to Sara about it. As close as we were, we'd never really had that kind of conversation. I kept it all bottled up until I found myself wandering aimlessly around the streets of Kentish Town at five in the morning. My depression had been affecting every aspect of my life, including my work. Later that day, I went to see Sara. We sat up on her roof garden together, and I broke down.

I was as honest as I could be, telling her that I wasn't

sure I could continue with the group and needed to step back for my sanity, that I had a child and responsibilities. Even then, I was telling myself, *pull yourself together, you stupid cow*. I was utterly drained. But I still didn't take a break because I simply didn't know how to. Instead, I carried on like a zombie, going to writing sessions while my head was somewhere else. I occasionally chipped in with a bit of writing, but Sara did the lion's share, and, as time went on, I knew she was feeling the pressure. I also knew that I wasn't being very supportive.

Eventually, I sat down and talked to Hills, who suggested that I speak to a therapist. It wasn't something I ever saw myself doing, but by then, I didn't feel like I had anything to lose. It was helpful in many ways. My therapist was as far removed from showbiz as you could get, and during our sessions, it felt a bit like I was sitting there, chatting with the kindest, most understanding granny in the world. As alien as the idea of talking about myself had first seemed, I was frank about how I felt. As it turned out, I didn't have that many sessions, but somehow I was able to let a whole lifetime of stuff go.

One of the things that came out of these sessions was that, for me, there were fundamental things that needed to change. I needed to find and maintain some sort of work/life balance, which is something that has continued to be relevant to me. Back then, the problem was how to go about that. In the music business, there was always something going on: a song to write, a photoshoot interview to do, strategies to plan, and producers to find. In Bananarama, we'd worked so hard for so long there didn't seem to be very much space for downtime.

When I started seeing Andrew Ridgeley, that balance began to change. The two of us spent weekends away together, sometimes in Cornwall, a place with which we both fell in love. Andrew and I had met a few times throughout the eighties, but back then he'd been living mostly in Monaco and Los Angeles. In December 1990, we met again at Simon Halfon's house and began dating. It wasn't all that serious to begin with, but our relationship grew, and culminated with him moving into my London home with me, Tom and the dogs. For me, at that time, he was a breath of fresh air. In previous relationships, I'd tended to take the helm when it came to organising and planning, or we'd never have ended up going anywhere or doing anything. I generally ended up paying for everything too. Andrew was different; he'd had his own successful career, and had his own money. He took me out on proper dates and organised trips away. I'd come home from work, and he'd say, 'Hey, I thought we could go here for the weekend, what do you think?'

As time went on, Andrew, Tom and I went to Cornwall regularly, and whenever we came home, Tom would be miserable all the way back, just like I'd been when returning from the seaside as a child. Up until then, I'd always sort of fitted motherhood in around my career. When I was pregnant with Tom, Bananarama were in their heyday; we were number one in the States with 'Venus', for God's sake! And I just carried on working my arse off once he was born, afraid to entirely give in to motherhood as if it were some kind of weakness. With hindsight, I think I probably had post-natal depression, but at the time I had no idea what that even was, so just kept on pushing through.

Initially, Andrew and I talked about the possibility of getting a holiday home in Cornwall, but one day I woke up and thought, why not move there permanently? Instead of working in London and grabbing the odd weekend in Cornwall, why not flip it? We could live there, and I could just come to London when I needed to for work.

Some of my friends were horrified at the idea of our plans to move.

'What are you going to do all day down there?' one friend asked. 'What are you going to talk about?'

'Something other than music, I hope,' was my answer.

—

SARA: After the world tour, we were both exhausted. True to form, we didn't take any time off, and there were no holidays. And, as we started planning the *Pop Life* album, I was shouldering most of the decision-making and running of the group. This increased my workload massively. It was bound to affect my health.

At my parents' house one day, I felt exhausted, unable to do anything other than just sit in a chair all day or lie down in the bedroom I had shared with my sister. There was a comfort in being in our childhood room, and that day, I felt like I could have laid there for ever. The following day, back at my place, our three dancers came over to run through the routines for an upcoming TV appearance. I remember watching them rehearse, but I just couldn't get off the sofa to join in, and they jokingly called me lazy. I was no better the following day, with a continuous headache, so I went to my doctor who assured me that I was just run down. But something didn't feel right. This was more than just feeling run down. I decided to contact a private emergency doctor who, when I arrived at his surgery, attached wires to me and asked me to walk on a treadmill, suggesting it might be a heart problem. Eventually, his conclusion was that I had severe flu and he sent me home with some Nurofen to bring down my high temperature.

That night, the headache became so excruciating I couldn't move. I felt as though my head was skewered to the pillow; it was terrifying. My boyfriend wasn't home, so I called Keren, and she rang 999. On arrival at the Whittington Hospital, my temperature had sky-rocketed, and I was given an injection of pethidine that literally wiped me out, completely suppressing the pain. It truly was the most welcome feeling imaginable. Still, I was more ill than I knew, and when, at one point, I tried to get out of bed, the world turned black, and I collapsed. After doctors performed a lumbar puncture to drain off some spinal fluid, I was finally diagnosed with meningitis.

During my week in hospital, Keren was right by my side and the nurses were fantastic, so attentive and kind. Once I was finally back home, Keren, Hills and my family helped nurse me back to health: shopping for food, cooking and making sure I had everything I needed. I, of course, realised how lucky I'd been.

Nothing in my life could compare to the utter joy I felt at the arrival of my daughter Alice a year later. She was the brightest star in my sky and is my heart and my soul. Fortunately, our workload wasn't as intense as it had been when Keren had Tom in the eighties, so I had plenty of time to spend with her, and my Labrador, Paddy. Of course I wouldn't have had it any other way. Alice made me deliriously happy, and being with her allowed me to focus on something other than Bananarama. It was heaven, a return to innocence.

There was a time when Alice was about two and I was working in New York. I was due to fly on to Japan when I had a phone call from her father saying that she was unwell. When I heard her little voice on the phone asking me to come home, I dropped everything and went. By that point in my life, it was a question of priorities: another TV appearance or mine and my child's happiness. No contest. I was fortunate that my parents and siblings adored looking after Alice, and Paddy too, while I was working away. Without their support, it would have been impossible, so I was genuinely grateful.

That following year, we started work on our sixth album, *Please Yourself*, which was to be our final album for London Records. It was at this time that we became friendly with Roland Mouret, a future fashion designer who ran Bar Freedom in Wardour Street. Roland was a handsome French man who everybody seemed to fall in love with. He was funny and super creative. We ended up collaborating with him on the artwork for our next few singles. He came up with the idea for the hourglass cut-outs that we used at the start of the video for 'Movin' On', and again on the record covers. He also came up with the idea of us as mermaids tattooed on a man's back, for the cover of *More, More, More*, although we dropped the man in the end.

For the 'Movin' On' video, we were introduced to designer Antony Price, who I'd seen in magazines as a school kid, with his friends Bryan Ferry and Jerry Hall. Now here he was making dresses for Keren and me. Instead of taking measurements when we went to his studio, he fashioned our bodies out of chicken wire. He wrapped the wire around us, leaving an opening at the back so we could step out of the shell before he closed it up with pliers. He had wire carcasses of various princesses, ladies and actresses stuffed under tables, and we dragged them out trying to guess who they were, although he would never divulge! 'Tone' was enormous fun, and his resulting creations were magnificent, bright-red affairs, that looked like something from the movie, *Gentlemen Prefer Blondes*.

15

GO YOUR OWN WAY

SARA: One day in 1994, Keren announced that she was relocating to Cornwall. Andrew, who'd retired in 1986, had bought a beautiful farmhouse in ninety acres of land, and off they went into the sunset. My childhood friend had moved 300 miles away.

For a while, Keren and I didn't see much of one another. I suppose it was only natural, given the distance, our new relationships, young children and the need to recharge our batteries. There were times, though, when I felt excluded from Keren's life, especially with our holidays together less frequent. I was still young and had a new baby, but the future of my career was uncertain. Being in a group together meant that Keren and I were dependent on one another for work.

There was a definite shift in the dynamic of our friendship over the next few years. For now, Keren had swapped London life for a set of golf clubs and a pair of wellies and seemed extremely content. I, on the other hand, wasn't quite ready for a quieter life.

I don't remember Keren discussing her feelings about the group in any depth, so to an extent, I was in the dark. She'd told me that Andrew had said he would support her decision to give up the band if she wanted to, but I didn't know if she was contemplating that. At the same time, I didn't realise how bad her depression was. I suppose I just thought she was going through a rough patch. I'd felt down myself on occasion, but my way of dealing with it was to throw myself into work rather than acknowledge I couldn't cope or seek help. The truth was, we really hadn't taken time out to discuss how either of us was coping mentally, and that was the problem. We'd been running at a hundred miles an hour for twelve years, neither of us realising that sometimes you just have to put the brakes on. Something has to give.

—

KEREN: For me, Cornwall was bliss. Andrew moved a few months before Tom and I did and I threw Tom an eighth birthday party for all his London friends at the Sobell Ice Rink, before moving to Cornwall on New Year's Eve of 1994. I think it rained every day for about three months. I didn't mind. Walking the dogs in lashing rain and wind was exhilarating, and I loved having the feeling of all that space and fresh air around me. The claustrophobia of London was a world away, and I wasn't in any rush to get back to it.

There was also a whole new social life to discover, albeit less hectic than the one I'd previously had. The first week there, I met Sue, who had kids of a similar age to Tom. The two of us immediately hit it off and we remain friends. Of course, Sara was still my best friend, but I didn't really have any other female friends in London, certainly not close ones. In Cornwall, I made friends quickly, and from all different walks of life. Quite a few, like us, had come from London to settle there.

Being part of a community was suddenly important to me. I had obviously had a great social life and loads of friends in London, but this was different. Not having to dress up or put dates in the diary, it was a lot easier and more relaxed, just a case of arriving at a friend's house or turning up at the local pub if I fancied some company. It was something I hadn't experienced since I was a child, and something I revelled in being part of. This was a place where people looked out for one another, and I guess that's one of the things that made me fall in love with it. That whole first summer in Cornwall was incredible. We were basking in a heatwave, so Sue and I took the kids to the beach every day. I finally felt like I could try to make up for some of the lost time with Tom, and I was happy for the first time in ages.

I still loved performing and making music, but I hated all the other stuff that went with it; I think Sara felt the same on that front. For me, being in Bananarama wasn't the be-all and end-all any more. I didn't want to stop altogether, but I very much needed a break.

At the time of my depression, and in those first years in Cornwall, I'll admit I didn't really care much about work. I threw myself into life in the country, and it made

With Bob, Keren's dad, at Matt's wedding.

me incredibly happy. The best part about it was that it was all so far removed from the music industry, and nobody seemed to care what I did or said. It was here that I realised the truth of something my dad always said: 'Happiness shouldn't be measured in terms of success or how much money you have. It's something much simpler.'

—

SARA: After a while, I started to get used to Keren's absence and acclimatised. I still loved London life and all it had to offer, and I may not have had my best friend, but I had my other close friends, and I was making some interesting new ones.

The nineties social scene was fabulous, and my closest friend at the time was David Thomas, or 'Soho

213

Dave' as I called him. He was a fashion stylist who I first met at a place called the Zebra Bar. Back then, he'd been the fashion editor of *GQ* and had asked Keren and me if we would be part of a photoshoot for the magazine. It was quite a curious shoot; Keren and I were both dressed in Versace on the steps of a glamorous hotel, with radio and television presenter Paul Gambaccini dressed as a bellboy.

David was the quintessential man about town. He knew everyone there was to know in London, so the two of us would be invited to the most incredible parties and fashion events. David introduced me to some amazing, and some not so amazing, friends. Our relationship was punctuated with laughter, and there was no limit to his generosity. On one occasion, he turned his vast loft apartment at London Bridge into what looked like a five-star Mayfair restaurant for Barbara Windsor's birthday party.

As well as our social escapades, David worked on several photoshoots and music videos for us. Whenever we arrived on set, the dressing room would be like Aladdin's cave, with the most fantastic designer and vintage clothes, rows of shoes and tables of jewellery. We called David 'the inexpensive jewel in our crown' because he was so generous with us.

One night, my friend Simon, who was doing the artwork for Paul Weller's records, invited Keren and me to see Paul play at the legendary Ronnie Scott's in Soho. Joining us that night was Noel Gallagher, who we'd previously met in Japan with his Oasis bandmates. We got on well with Noel so it was good to see him again. Oasis had just released *Definitely Maybe* and were on the verge of becoming the biggest band in the UK. We all enjoyed a great night, until it was time to go home. It was late and Soho was all but deserted, so trying to find a cab back to Simon's flat in St John's Wood (pre-Uber) was a nightmare. After waving frantically at a couple of passing taxis with no light on, Noel flagged down a refuse lorry on its late-night inner-city rounds. The refuse men recognised Noel, Keren and me straight away, and after Noel explained our plight, they said they were more than happy to give us all a lift home. It was pretty surreal travelling up-front in a dustcart, chatting away to Noel and his then-girlfriend Meg.

Once we arrived at Simon's place, they followed us up to the flat. Simon produced a camera and photos were taken. After a few beers, Keren took it upon herself to ask them to leave, escorting them to the door. On her return, careering around the living room to some late-night tunes, she crashed into an antique table that had belonged to Simon's mother and snapped the legs off.

Throughout the nineties, some of the clubs we frequented became more 'sophisticated', meaning you had to reserve a table and pay £150 for a bottle of vodka. One of the perks of being a celebrity is that we never had to pay to get in or buy drinks. Having said that, I don't think we did those things in our pre-celebrity days either. Other clubs became more rave-orientated, housed in huge cavernous warehouses like Bagley's and

The Cross in King's Cross, Fabric in Farringdon, East London, and The Ministry of Sound in Southwark, where superstar DJs like Paul Oakenfold, David Morales and Roger Sanchez played. This was the genesis of celebrity DJ culture. Even our London Records A&R guy Pete Tong was now a renowned DJ, and played at Ministry. Keren and I were comfortable in any and all of these different settings. We flitted from one club to another, enjoying the varied nightlife.

One of mine and David's favourite clubs at the time was Kabaret in Upper John Street, W1, which was the most brilliant fun. My friend Charlotte was maître d' there. I can't remember where we met but Charlotte was an absolute gem and a brilliant dancer. On nights at Kabaret, she and I would arrive early and sit in the corner booth, which overlooked the dance floor. It was a tiny club, managed by our friend, Ronnie, who, as luck would have it, lived across the road from me, assuring me a lift home at the end of the night. From our vantage point, Charlotte and I would sip cocktails and watch everyone arrive. It was a real celeb hangout. On the far side of the club would be the likes of Guy Ritchie, Tom Parker Bowles, and Tara Palmer-Tomkinson. On the other side was everyone from Chris Lowe, Ewan McGregor, Jude Law and Johnny Lee Miller to Stella McCartney, Pharrell and, occasionally, gallery owner Tim Jefferies, who has always been the most hilarious company. A few hours into the evening, there would be a cabaret on the tiny stage. The most vivid in my memory is 'Geordie Porn Star', who performed an exercise routine and sang in German. It was a night not to be missed, and Keren would sometimes drive the 600-mile round trip from Cornwall just to attend. It sometimes seemed like she was leading a double life, and it must have been exhausting.

Whenever she visited London, Keren stayed with me. We'd hang out, go clubbing and do what work needed to be done. We've always had the best fun when we're together, which is something that has never changed. Our touring band members have often said that they always know where we are in an airport or a building because they can hear our laughter before they see us. We can still make each other laugh until we can't breathe or see through the tears. It's been like that ever since we were at school when one of us would have to stand up in class to read a passage from a book, while the other rustled a Wagon Wheels wrapper to throw them off.

During this time, my partner Bassey and I set up a small studio at home where we began writing and recording songs. Our friends, Paul Swaby and Joe Rice, would sometimes come over and work on tracks with us. On some evenings, Bruno and Paul would join us for dinner. Bruno would cook one of his Italian specialities, and we'd all sit around the table like one big happy family, complete with kids and dogs. I enjoyed this productive time, which was stimulating and good for my soul. Writing and creating is an intrinsic part of who I am, so I certainly wasn't about to kick back and retire just yet.

We were prolific, too, working with various songwriters from the dance scene that Bassey introduced me to. I recorded a few Ibiza-style tracks that made it onto various compilations. It wasn't just the songwriting element I enjoyed; I loved getting involved in production too. I'd become quite adept at recording, building up tracks and arranging vocals. For me, the entire process was satisfying. Working alongside someone supportive and talented was just what I needed.

My manager at the time, Albert Samuel, arranged for me to work with different writing partners and it initially felt strange to turn up at studios alone to work with people I'd never met. I'd been used to a certain way of working, which was to discuss the direction of the music, take away a basic drum beat and chords and come up with a top line and lyrics at home in my own time. With one particular songwriting team it was a little more awkward. When I arrived at the dreary rehearsal room, there was a quick introduction before the guy started plonking away on the piano waiting for me to come up with a melody right off the bat. It didn't feel right. But I wrote a huge amount of songs in this period of time, some of which made it onto our future albums.

However much recording on my own was quite liberating, I missed Keren's input and the way we bounce off each other when it comes to writing. She has a brilliant musical ear and we love arranging songs together. Songwriting and recording is definitely my favourite part of being in the group.

Albert Samuel had started out as our live agent. On

paper, we were chalk and cheese, but we got on like a house on fire, and he was a good businessman. He thought Keren and I were a little eccentric – in fact, totally mad – but he adored us, and the feeling was mutual. He's hilarious – a really chilled, lovely guy. He had the idea to put us in the studio with producer Gary Miller. Gary was collaborating with a couple of songwriters, and together we wrote and recorded *Ultra Violet*. We were without a record deal at this point so Albert decided to license the record to a very successful Japanese company called AVEX who paid for the recording. He then licensed it to the US and the rest of the world apart from the UK. We flew out to Japan to debut the album and record a track with a popular Japanese artist. Apart from the financial benefits of the licensing deals it was great to still be able to write and record music fifteen years into our career and I think at this point we were both of the opinion that success is more about being creative and happy than a chart position.

With this album we found ourselves travelling the world, once again performing short live sets everywhere from European music festivals to Grand Prix and US casinos.

We were invited by the UK government to play live at the spectacular handover of Hong Kong to China on 1 July 1997, and at several powerboat races in Dubai and Abu Dhabi, where we received the five-star treatment. On one trip, Keren and I were taken through the crystal-clear waters to an island on a luxury yacht.

Once on the island, we were served a delicious array of traditional food, and let loose on dune buggies and camels.

Keith Cox was our tour manager on this trip, a sweet, funny redhead. He and our dancers had to follow us on a small speedboat and were dropped off as close to shore as was possible. As Keith was disembarking, he misjudged the jetty and landed knee-deep in a grey silt, which was quite impossible to move in. In the forty-five-degree heat, he was already as red as a lobster, but once he'd extracted himself from the silt, he looked as though he was wearing grey stockings. It was the most hilarious sight, and we were all weeping with laughter. To top it all, I managed to capture it on film.

In Thailand with Coxy.

KEREN: Keith, or Coxy as he came to be known, came on many a trip with us, including one to Bangkok where we all decided to go for a Thai massage. We arrived at an authentic massage parlour, which had one big room that could be separated into cubicles. Still, as we all knew one another, we left the curtains open. Dressed only in the sarongs we'd been given, we settled onto our mattresses with the boys opposite the girls. The masseuses were tiny but strong, and the session ended with us all being stretched upwards with our arms in a tight grip behind our heads. At this point, unfortunately for him, Keith's sarong burst open, leaving him totally exposed in red-faced glory, with us laughing at him. His agony was prolonged as he tried to

Sightseeing in Tokyo with Carmine Canuso and Keith Cox.

make a grab for something to cover his modesty. However, the tiny but strong woman performing his massage wasn't letting go of his hands before she was good and ready.

Albert also booked us on a couple of shows in Russia, which was somewhere we'd never been. I've never experienced cold like winter in Moscow. Nothing could have prepared us for the biting winds in Red Square, where we stepped out of a Barbie-pink limo, which stood out like a sore thumb in the snow. St Basil's Cathedral looked stunning all right, but we were bloody freezing and succumbed, out of pure desperation, to buying typically Russian fur hats from a street vendor. They did the trick at the time, but even now I'm concerned that I may have briefly worn somebody's beloved pet on my head.

In Russia, we were slightly unnerved by the fact the promoter had provided us with two armed bodyguards, who were reputedly ex-KGB. They came everywhere with us – and I mean *everywhere* – but we had no clue as to why it was necessary. Out at a club one night, both Sara and I had to visit the ladies, as you do.

'Don't worry, we'll be fine on our own,' didn't wash with our minders, and we were duly accompanied through the door of the loo. Imagine our embarrassment to find that, inside, a 1970s-style beaded curtain was the only thing safeguarding our dignity – and it wasn't even slightly discreet.

We played an enormous event at the Olympic stadium before heading for St Petersburg, taking the train instead of flying. What a great way to see the countryside, we thought, imagining scenes from *Doctor Zhivago* or *Anna Karenina*. As it turned out, it was so misty we couldn't even see our hands in front of our faces, and the train was deathly slow and freezing. We were offered some soup, which had all the allure of tepid washing-up water, and stiff, coarse blankets, which we huddled beneath.

I knew what St Petersburg looked like from photos and films, but when you're standing in front of it, the sheer scale of the Winter Palace is breathtaking. We only had half a day to see what probably should have taken a week. Still, we enjoyed a whistle-stop, private tour around the must-see exhibits in the Hermitage, including the glorious Fabergé egg collection.

These trips were all such brilliant fun. In the decade between 1989 and 1998, we hadn't toured with a band, but with Albert at the helm, we'd ended up playing some wonderfully unexpected places and some incredible out-of-the-ordinary shows. We weren't away for long periods of time, which meant we could be at home with the kids more, but it also felt as if we saw more of the world than we had on the hectic travels we had undertaken during the previous decade.

I'm sure Albert found the two of us exasperating at times. He was the straightest man on earth and no matter where we went, he'd end up in a club or bar surrounded by a bevy of beautiful women. At one point, Sara and I thought he needed a change, so finding ourselves in New York on his fortieth, we took him to the iconic drag restaurant, Lucky Cheng's, in the East Village, where all the waiting staff were gender-ambiguous. We revelled in putting poor Albert in the most uncomfortable of positions, which, on this occasion, included getting one of the drag waitresses to sit on his lap and sing 'Happy Birthday', while he squirmed with embarrassment. After dinner, a guy from the record company whisked us all off on a surprise visit to The Vault. Once a notorious S&M club in the Meatpacking District, the club had now become a bit of a tourist attraction. On entering, our first vision was of an older man, naked apart from his Jesus sandals, swinging on a sex-chair suspended from the ceiling. Albert was horrified, but the rest of us casually sat at the bar and ordered a drink. Spotting some latex curtains, Sara and I dared Albert to go and find out what was going on behind them. He bravely took up the challenge, but by the time he came back, his expression was one of such extreme shock that we all howled with laughter. Unfortunately for us, laughing wasn't the done thing and, having drawn attention to ourselves, a staff member sidled over, cautioning us that The Vault was a participation club, and if we weren't going to join in, we should perhaps leave. All things considered, and given what Albert had witnessed behind the latex curtains, this appeared to be the most sensible idea and we all slinked out before we got into any further trouble. We ended up dancing the night away at the Palladium's gay night.

Poor Albert had to relive the embarrassment all over again when Sara and I repeated the story to Jocelyn Brown – who Albert also managed – at lunch the next day.

—

SARA: Throughout this period, we kept running into other artists around the world, and realised that this kind of gig was what a lot of people did when they weren't on TV all the time. Indeed, it was performing these shows with Albert that gave us both the bug to start doing more live work again.

—

KEREN: Around this time, we started working with PR guru Connie Filippello, who was also George Michael's PR, among many others. Sara and I did shoots for *Hello!*, which were arranged by Connie, and she joined us on a fair few trips abroad in the nineties. One night, she joined us for an auction at Christie's, in aid of the Terrence Higgins Trust, along with George Michael and his boyfriend, Kenny. I'd always felt that Sara was Connie's favourite of the two of us, and had been from our first meeting. That night, we ended up laughing about it, with me recalling the time she'd presented Sara with an exquisite top, one evening in Paris.

'Try it on, darling, it's Versace,' she'd said.

Nothing for me, then?

On another occasion, Connie was talking to us about the actor, Rupert Everett.

'You must meet him, darling, he would love you,' she told Sara.

Turning to me, she then said, 'He'd quite like you!' Then back to Sara. 'But he would *love* you, darling!'

The final straw came at a Mariah Carey party, which Connie had organised – a masked ball, to be precise. Sara and I had been working all day and turned up at the do with our stylist and friend, David Thomas. We had no masks to don, but the paps were there, and Connie wanted a photo. Quick as a flash, she threw her arms around Sara, adorning her with a glamorous, feather-trimmed mask, worthy of the fanciest Venetian ball.

Turning her attention to me, she said, 'Put the mask on, darling,' and promptly handed me a full-face gimp mask.

David and I collapsed in hysterics on the pavement – what else could I do?

Dear Connie – she was, and is, hilarious!

It wasn't just Connie who seemed to favour Sara either. At the auction night, Sara ended up with an envy-inducing designer handbag, generously presented to her by Kenny.

Also present at the auction that night was artist Tracey Emin, who had donated some of her artwork. Once the sale was over, we all ended up at The Ivy for supper and drinks.

Looking back now, I remember so much good stuff happened during that period. Now we weren't living in each other's pockets, when we did see one another, we made the most of our time together. Yes, it was different, but the bond was no less strong. My friendship with Sara has always been something that transcends Bananarama, but sometimes, the two things can get so intertwined that it's hard to know where one starts and the other one finishes. On occasion over the years, I have relied on Sara to keep the group going behind the

'Put the mask on darling.'

scenes, but being in Bananarama is essentially part of who I am and a part of our friendship. After a few blips, the nineties turned out to be a great decade and a period of natural and necessary change and progression in both our careers and our friendship. That set us up for the next twenty years, probably my favourite period since the excitement of the early eighties.

16

THE GENTLE-MAN

KEREN: One of the upsides of not having such a crazily busy schedule was that it allowed us to take some much-needed holidays. Sara had been to Ibiza on holiday before. Still, I had previously only been to perform with her and Jacquie on a strange TV show, where we ended up filming on a boat trip to Formentera along with Italian star, Sabrina. We'd watched in amazement from the beach as she frolicked topless in the sea with a politician.

Anyway, I decided it was high time I went there just for fun, so Sara and I booked into Pikes hotel, famous for being the hotel featured in Wham's 'Club Tropicana' video.

On this trip, we were joined by our friend, Peter Loraine. When he was fifteen, Peter had started writing an unofficial Bananarama fanzine called *True Confessions*. At the time, we had a couple of sacks of unopened fan mail that needed attention. Hillary contacted Peter and asked him to run the official fan club. Later, Peter started to work for the big pop mags of the day. By now, we were all hanging out as friends, and there was clubbing and many parties at his London flat when he started working for Universal Music. A few years down the line, in 2009, Peter signed us up to his own label, Fascination Records, on hearing our new song, 'Love Comes'. I suppose it may sound odd, becoming so close to someone who started as a fan, but our friendship transcended that, and Peter became someone I felt I could trust to have our best interests at heart. Over the years, I've stayed at his place and sometimes, while we're dancing around his kitchen, I'll say, 'Wow! This is a great track, who is it?'

'It's you!' he'll say. 'It's Bananarama!'

On this, my first Ibiza holiday, Peter introduced us to his friend, Hywel, who managed DJs and had a car which we christened 'the golden chariot'. We were off and running. Different clubs were best on different days, and I think we went to them all. Daytime clubbing was a brand-new experience, but we embraced it wholeheartedly. In fact, within a couple of days of arriving, it felt completely normal to dance the day away at Space and then carry on through the night. These were hedonistic times, and we could both let loose without worrying that we had to get up and work the next day. All we had to do was lie by the pool and top up our tans, eat, drink and, of course, dance. We were in our thirties and having fun like teenagers – perhaps catching up on some of the carefree youth we'd missed out on during the early days of Bananarama, fifteen years before. Of course, we'd all enjoyed that ride, but there was always a recording session, TV appearance, interview or photoshoot looming and there hadn't really been time for holidays. Now, all I had to worry about was staying happy and looking tanned and lovely. After all, this was probably going to be the last time I went out in a miniskirt!

There were moments when it all got a bit much for me, but I simply refused to give in. On one particular night, while we were dancing on podiums in the VIP area in Pasha, I suddenly felt sick. It had been a fabulous night up until then: with Roger Sanchez and David Morales on the decks, the atmosphere and music were electric. Sara could see I was slowly going green but was loath to get down off her podium to assist. In the end, though, she helped me down off the table and whisked me out through the fire escape to 'get some air'.

'Do you want to go back to the hotel?' she asked.

'Absolutely not, I'm fine!' I replied, and we swiftly returned to our tabletops to continue dancing till dawn.

We went back for a repeat performance a couple of years later, staying at Es Vive, which was a stylish, art deco hotel next to the beach and close to town. We planned on this trip being slightly more chilled than the previous one, but as we walked into the hotel, it seemed as though half the people around the pool were shouting and waving at us. There was such an eclectic mix of people around, from Howard Donald of Take That, who was DJing, and Ritchie from Five, to various actors and even hairdressers we knew. As is always the case, the fear of being photographed in an unflattering light while sunbathing loomed heavy, so we generally rolled up our towels and snuck off to a quiet corner away from everyone else. In hindsight, we shouldn't have worried because we both looked great.

—

SARA: Sometime in the early nineties we were headlining a festival in Japan and The Prodigy were on the same bill. I was a fan of their early tracks, 'Charley' and 'Out of Space', which had been played a lot on MTV. During the festival, AVEX, the event's organisers and the label we were signed to, threw a big dinner after which each act took to the stage and introduced themselves. We had to walk past the table where The Prodigy were sitting, and I was waiting for them to make some comment as they were the new kids on the block. I couldn't have been more wrong; they were all lovely. At the after-show party, Leeroy and Keith especially couldn't have been more complimentary. We laughed all night and spent the next ten days hanging out and clubbing in Tokyo. They even ended up travelling around the city with us in our VIP bus. This was the start of the sweetest friendship between the four of us, and especially for Keith Flint and me. Keith was the most beautiful, kind soul, and, as Bruno Tonioli said when I introduced them, 'He has the face of an angel.' At that point, Keith still had his lovely, long hair.

Back in London, Keren and I welcomed Keith and Leeroy into our world. They would drive up from Essex in Keith's clapped-out car, and we'd cab it into Soho, often starting at our friend Aldo Zilli's restaurant before moving to various parties and clubs: Kabaret, Met Bar, Ten Room, and Chinawhite being some of our favourites. With Keren in Cornwall much of the time, Keith became my man-about-town and best friend, and we shared some hilarious times. He'd often just crash at my house, and the two of us would lie on the floor in the dark listening to Pink Floyd's *Dark Side of the Moon*. We were always laughing, with me referring to him as 'stupid boy' in the style of Captain Mainwaring reprimanding young Pike in *Dad's Army*. He loved it, and the phrase stuck.

After The Prodigy hit the big time, he invited me to Great Dunmow in Essex, to see an old run-down property that he was thinking of buying. He was passionate about the history of the place and the prospect of its renovation. This beautiful farmhouse would eventually become his home, where he lived up until his death. When he wasn't touring and had time to relax, I would often drive down with my daughter Alice and stay for the weekend. He bought her a bike so we could all go for country rides and then head to his local pub for lunch. Alice was in her element when she discovered one of his barns had an enormous jacuzzi.

Keith loved animals and had a pack of dogs that would surround our car to greet us when we arrived: four vizslas and a red setter, all male, and one female, a black Lab called Strudel who we adored. We would take them for walks in the grounds where he had giant wooden carved seats; it felt like something out of *Alice in Wonderland*. Leeroy and his sister Sharon would often join us there. Keith would cook delicious dinners for us all, introducing me to the delights of tofu for the first time.

On one occasion, while Alice and I were up near the pond where his ducks and geese lived, the dogs got loose and terrorised the poor creatures, eventually killing one of the geese. It was the most horrifying sight, and Alice was understandably distraught. Afterwards, Keith took Alice and the goose up to some shrub land and placed the bird gently down, covering it with leaves. He told Alice that she was just sleeping, which made her feel better.

Keith adored Alice. If I was having a lie-in on a Saturday morning, I'd often hear the two of them chatting, and Alice singing in his vegetable garden. She would help him feed his two pot-bellied pigs, then they'd jump on his motorbike and ride around the farm and up over the hills into the distance. Alice was sublimely happy and said she felt like she was in a movie.

Sometimes, the three of us would go down to Cornwall and visit Keren, and Keith would arrive in the local pub, with his green hair, tattoos and piercings, to gasps from the locals. He'd just had 'Inflicted' tattooed on his stomach, which he showed everybody in the pub, and somehow the ice was broken. They loved him.

—

KEREN: At one point, Keith even considered buying a house in Cornwall. I did a recce of suitable homes, and then he came down for a week to visit them. The reaction of the sellers was hilarious. Keith had a Mohican at the time – green, of course – and most of the would-be vendors found it impossible to conceal their horror when they opened the door and saw him standing there. Tom became the coolest kid in the school when Keith drove him to football club in his yellow TVR, screeching into the car park with a handbrake turn.

Keith just had a knack of winning everyone over. We always said he could 'light up a room with his smile'. He came to Cornwall for Christmas one year, with Sara, Alice, David Thomas and members of Andrew's family, fitting in perfectly and playing all the usual Christmas Day games. I feel incredibly sad that he's not with us any more, and that towards the end of his life we didn't see as much of him, as we always seemed to be so busy working. Just a few days before his death, Sara and I decided that it had been much too long and we needed to call him. As it turned out, we were too late, and we both regret not getting to see him. It's one of those heartbreaking times in life when you think, *if only*.

—

SARA: We saw The Prodigy play live many times in their career. When they played Knebworth, Maxim dragged Keren and me on stage from the wings, where we danced with gay abandon in our flip flops. On another occasion, while Keith was in full performance mode, flying over the audience on a wire, he spotted Keren's son at the sound desk and stopped to say 'All right, Tom!' and then carried on flying. They really were the most awesome band, and Keith was the most awesome man.

17

AFTER THE RAIN COMES THE SUN

KEREN: We'd always resisted doing tours with other artists, but as the nineties drew to a close, we were itching to get back on stage with a live band. When we were offered the Club Sandwich Tour, along with Belinda Carlisle, Heaven 17 and Culture Club, it seemed the perfect way for us to get back into touring. For Club Sandwich, we shared a band with Belinda and played arenas up and down the UK in the run-up to Christmas.

It was great fun having other artists to hang out with, and we had a few raucous group nights out together. Belinda was always great company, and over the next few years, we did shows all over the world with her, particularly in Asia. Together, we'd sip cocktails in glamorous hotels and bars while she regaled us with the most fantastically unfiltered gossip. As well as playing Singapore, Hong Kong and Bangkok, we played a few nights in a casino in the Genting resort in Malaysia, where the venue and hotel were one and the same, and, joy of joys, there was a nightclub in the basement. Sara and I have always enjoyed a hotel nightclub on our travels over the decades, although sadly, it seems to have become less of a thing these days.

Getting back to doing live work ignited something in us. Having a band behind us was brilliant and something we'd missed. Nothing beats a proper show. For me, this was a real turning point. Bananarama was once again something I was enjoying. We were on the road, making music and having a fantastic time, just as it should be!

—

SARA: With the millennium fast approaching, I found myself in a new relationship. He was a musician from New York and consequently I started spending more time there. On one of my early trips, I caught a cab from JFK to his apartment, feeling the same excitement and energy that I'd always felt arriving in New York, crossing the bridges and seeing the famous skyline drawing closer. I didn't take much notice of the area we were driving through, but it seemed pretty nice and my boyfriend's apartment had a doorman who welcomed us – just like they did in the movies.

For the first few days of my visit, he was finishing off an album in a studio downtown, so we arranged to meet at a coffee shop later and he gave me the address. I jumped in the shower of the very small bathroom, which reminded me of Carrie Bradshaw's bathroom in *Sex and the City*, old with white tiles. Having showered,

I tried to open the door, flying into a complete claustrophobic panic when it wouldn't budge. The bathroom window leading to the outside world was tiny, and I couldn't even push it upwards to cry for help. Eventually, I managed to escape and caught a cab to our meeting place, but once there, I ended up hanging around for what seemed like an eternity. I tried calling his mobile but, as it later transpired, he had no signal in the studio. For the second time that day, panic descended, as it occurred to me that I was in the middle of New York, not knowing where the studio, or, indeed, my boyfriend was. On top of that, I hadn't bothered to take note of his home address.

There was huge relief when he eventually turned up, and I'm happy to report that subsequent visits weren't quite as harrowing. In fact, arriving there for the millennium celebrations was thrilling. Times Square was packed, with everything lit up like a Christmas tree, all set to the familiar soundtrack of New York cabs, honking their horns. We made our way across town in the freezing cold and celebrated in a beautiful restaurant where my boyfriend seemed to know everybody. It was wonderful to spend New Year somewhere different, rather than the usual chasing around from one party to the next across London.

In early 2000, Bruno and I were lounging around in his garden, discussing life, love and where we were at in our careers. He happened to mention a French recording artist he'd been working with. It all sounded quite interesting, so I asked Bruno if he thought the artist's

Sara's birthday weekend in Paris, Christmas market on the Champs-Élysées.

With the Pascals and Alice at the Palace of Versailles.

producer, Pascal Caubet, would be interested in working with Keren and me. After all, we'd had lots of success in France. We still visited several times a year, appearing on some of the big TV shows and at festivals around the country. Keren had even been asked out by the legendary Charles Aznavour! I always enjoyed spending time in France, especially in Paris. At one point, it was almost like a second home to me.

After our chat, Bruno spoke to Pascal, who said he'd very much like to work with us. Just like that, we were off on a new adventure. Some of the recordings took place in Paris, which was a bonus. The resulting album was *Exotica*, which we signed to M6 Music – part of the most profitable private French TV channel. The album was released exclusively in France, and the videos for the two singles were shot in Paris and Barcelona. We viewed our 'French project' as a chance to get back in the studio and write songs.

Paris was also the place where we met our now dear friends, Pascal Maurice and Pascal Morniroli. Pascal Maurice had set up a Bananarama website long before we had even thought about it and introduced himself to us on the set of the Parisian TV show, *Toutes Les Chansons Ont Une Histoire*, on which we were appearing. The unofficial website was so good that we asked him to continue officially. I adore Paris and the Pascals so much that I have spent three of my birthdays there with them. They are also extremely well versed in art, culture and cuisine, so make the perfect hosts.

—

SARA: In 2004, I met a friend at a film reception who happened to mention that an acquaintance of hers was setting up a record label. Augusto Gentili was a wealthy Italian who was passionate about music, and just a few weeks later, we were meeting at his home in Harley Street. This location proved quite handy in the months that followed as Alice's school was only a few doors down, so I was able to arrange meetings around the school run. Augusto was charming and very enthusiastic and, over the coming weeks, we discussed our plans and the direction we wanted the next album to take, eventually signing to his burgeoning label, A&G. After a few false starts with personnel, he ultimately assembled a strong music industry team to work with, which included Jemma Crowe and Brian Harris. We were all buzzing with ideas; this felt like the most cohesive plan we'd had in a long time. Most excitingly, we were to fly to Sweden to work with the production house, Murlyn, which had had great success working with the likes of Britney Spears, Jennifer Lopez, Janet Jackson and Madonna.

We arrived in Stockholm during winter, early 2005, and stayed in a very cool, bohemian-style hotel, full of hip young people. Every morning, we'd head down to breakfast in the fifties-style coffee bar, which was buzzing with conversation, people on laptops and newspapers strewn across tables. The car would collect us, and we'd drive through the city to the studios, which were amid a snow-covered forest. Sweden does snow exceptionally well; it can be six feet high, but roads are clear, and day-to-day life continues unimpeded. As we drove through the trees approaching the studio complex, I could see people cross-country skiing far off in the distance. Breathing in the cold air, I felt a sense of calm; it was almost as if I knew this was where I was meant to be, and that everything was going to work out well. And it did! We worked with two teams of writers, the first being a duo known as Korpi and Blackcell. Henrik Korpi was an absolute nutter, in a good way – we'd definitely met a kindred spirit – and Mathias Johansson, known as Blackcell, was a super-talented musician and all-round lovely guy. We gelled instantly, and songwriting was inspiring. As with Youth, we were free to experiment with all sorts of ideas. We worked hard and laughed a lot and ultimately came up with what might be my favourite song, 'Look on the Floor'.

At weekends, the four of us would head into town. There was one club night at an enormous hotel – it was like an opera house – very ornate with chandeliers and a lot of wood panelling. There were loads of different rooms, all jam-packed with people, and throughout the evening, we kept losing one other. At one point, Korpi and I found ourselves ducking underneath the bar to reach the other part of the building in search of the other two, and being severely reprimanded for doing so. After many hours of dancing and pushing our way through crowds to the bathroom we decided to call it a night. We arrived back at the hotel thinking it was still

The making of the 'Move in My Direction' video, Las Vegas, 2005.

reasonably early, so couldn't understand why the staff were asking us to keep our raucous laughter down. That was until we realised it was about 4 a.m., and with a recording session booked for the next day, we decided it might be best if we headed off to bed.

Our songwriting session the next day was with David Clewett and Ivar Lisinski, who were two talented young writers collectively known as Mute 8. From the minute they started putting a backing track together, I knew the results were going to be great. Tired from the night before, with our heads spinning with the memory of it, Keren and I recounted the tale in lyrics. 'Move in My Direction' was written in twenty minutes and included the lyric: 'should have caught a taxi, should have gone straight home!'

We returned to Stockholm in the spring and summer months to finish the album *Drama*, which has become a fan favourite, as well as a favourite of mine. In 'Move in My Direction' and 'Look on the Floor' it gave us two more UK chart hits and they also made it into the Billboard dance charts, with 'Look on the Floor' reaching number two. We were thrilled with its success especially after twenty-six years in the business.

The video for 'Move in My Direction' was filmed in Las Vegas by director Phil Griffin. Part of the backdrop of the shoot was the Neon Boneyard, way out in the desert. It's the most amazing place, housing all the old signs and memorabilia from clubs, bars and hotels from Vegas's bygone era.

Call time for the shoot was 6 a.m. and, as per usual,

Keren, myself and Jemma were there on the dot. The crew and the rest of the entourage didn't rock up until 6.45 a.m., having factored in 'pop star punctuality' – i.e. invariably late. As you can imagine, it wasn't the best start to the day. Still, we had a great team working on the video: Duke Snyder on make-up and hair duties, Paul Roberts on staging, and stylist Sinead McKeefry, who was brilliant. The video for 'Look on the Floor' was truly inspired, directed by Tim Royes who is sadly no longer with us. I love its simple, clean lines – it's just very cool. The hair blowing in the wind scenes are courtesy of the hairstylist on his knees with a hair dryer. We were also treated to a Kirby wire experience for

another shot, which saw us flung high into the air in our metallic leggings with capes billowing. It may look like fun but it was extremely hot and uncomfortable. There is a wonderful and hilarious pastiche of the video on YouTube by a couple of guys from Seattle, The Bears: Bearnanarama v Bananarama.

—

KEREN: For me, the whole experience of making *Drama* was like waking from a siesta. I felt invigorated and positive about the future. After recording most of the album in Sweden, we finished a couple of tracks with writer/producer Ian Masterson, and this was the start of a beautiful friendship. Neither Ian nor I can remember exactly where we first met, but we think it might have been on a night out at Kabaret. Sara had already met Ian, during the period when I was in Cornwall and she was collaborating with various other songwriters. The first time we were in the studio together was to record 'Your Love Is Like a Drug', a song that Sara had written with Ian and his writing partner, Terry Ronald, which eventually appeared on *Drama*. We went on to write 'Feel for You' together and Ian could have easily filled a whole album with outtakes of our laughter and, in my case, appalling language when I got the lyrics wrong – even though they were pinned up on the wall in front of me.

—

SARA: We have a great friendship with Ian (and his partner Dan). He has the biggest heart; he is kind, trustworthy and hilarious. Aside from that we have the most brilliant working relationship. Writing and recording is creative and easy, with no egos. We have written three albums together and he has been incredibly supportive of us throughout.

—

KEREN: I'm not sure we've ever enjoyed studio time as much as we do with Ian. He and Bananarama are a match made in heaven, and it feels as far from working as you can get. In fact, since the making of our album *Viva*, in 2009, we have worked almost exclusively with Ian. We work well as a team, and he's never fazed by our many demands to change the tracks or keys or to bin stuff if it's not working. Typical studio days involve Sara and me going in and having coffee, singing our ideas to Ian, getting the main vocal lines down, and then breaking for a lunch of spicy salami and gorgonzola panini with a glass of red wine at the local Italian deli. After that, we head back to the studio, all ready to improve our new composition and work on the harmonies and countermelodies with fresh ears, often accompanied by studio disco-dogs, Marilyn and Martha. With Ian, we're comfortable enough to let loose with gay abandon and try anything. On *Viva*, we recorded a cover of Simon and Garfunkel's 'The Sound of Silence'. Sara and I had loved the duo's lush harmonies since we were kids, back when we were singing into the cassette recorder. We got quite emotional during the recording, layering on more and more harmonies – we didn't want to stop.

Every time we start a new album with Ian, the plan is to make it 'disco', but it inevitably veers off into whatever inspires us while we're working. Maybe the next one.

Ian has been enlisted in the role of tour manager on many a trip – just for the hell of it – and we could probably fill another book with our late-night conversations in random hotels. We've worked with him on the live arrangements for years, including the reunion tour, when he once again breathed new life into the early songs, so we never tire of performing them. Although saying that, 'I Want You Back' will always be the exception. It's the one song I'd be happy never to perform again, but a firm fan favourite.

For the launch of *Viva*, we performed the complete album live at the Garage in Islington, especially for fans. We also played the Isle of Wight Festival, which was a big deal for us, acknowledging us as a credible live act. Knowing that we could hold our own on a big festival stage gave us a newfound confidence.

Over the next few years, we didn't stop, playing various shows and special events all over the world. In 2006, we toured in South Africa with Will Young and Ronan Keating. We'd had success there but had never visited, so this was exciting. The trip was indeed memorable, mostly for the right reasons, but there were a few disasters along the way too.

Almost from the word go both Sara and I had terrible stomachs, existing on Imodium, which always seemed to wear off just before showtime. Suffice to say that this resulted in a couple of delayed starts to the set. On top of that, Sara got the worst food poisoning I have ever witnessed. She contracted it after a show at a sports ground when we trotted backstage to sample the local catering, which may have been hanging around a little too long in the intense heat. I plumped for a greasy cheese sandwich, while Sara went for the healthy option of a salad – only, as it turned out, not so healthy.

The ensuing hours were horrendous with Sara intermittently giving her best Linda Blair in *The Exorcist* impression. Somehow, she soldiered on through a travel day. Flying to Pretoria on a small prop plane was scary enough, without having to sit right at the back of it to be within easy reach of the loo.

This wasn't the worst flight of the trip. That award goes to our trip to Durban, where we landed in a thunderstorm with such turbulence it was like riding a rollercoaster. Generally, during moments of abject terror on planes, Sara and I console ourselves with the fact that nobody else on board seems bothered by the bumps. In this instance, such consolation was futile. As the plane plunged sharply before rising back up, seemingly at a right angle, the cabin crew held onto one another, screaming. The whole flight screamed, including me, until Sara punched me. It's little wonder we hate flying and always expect the worst.

Still, it wasn't all bad. In between shows, sunbathing and the regular, essential 'comfort breaks', we got to play with lion cubs at a safari park, although . . .

'They're a little bit scabby,' I commented to one of the keepers.

'Yes, they have ringworm,' the keeper calmly informed us.

We raced to the toilets to scrub our hands, only to discover there was no water. Sadly, that did take the shine off the day a little.

The shows, however, were wonderful, culminating in a big award ceremony, hosted by Jane Seymour, who was as charming as she is beautiful.

—

SARA: We first met Marc Carey in October 2008. He was the Dublin-born European marketing director of Hard Rock and responsible for putting together their live shows. He invited us to play at the Women in Rock concert at the Albert Hall in 2009 supporting the Caron Keating Foundation, which is a cancer fundraising charity set up by Caron's mother, Gloria Hunniford.

Jocelyn Brown was one of the backing vocalists in the incredible thirteen-piece band that played behind us at the show, complete with brass section and the guitarist and bass player from the Average White Band. During rehearsals for the show, we found ourselves having to point out the timing of the backing vocals for 'Love in the First Degree' to her. I have to say she took that song to a whole other dimension. We must have been a bit reserved in rehearsals because on the night, post a fantastic show, members of the band came up to us saying, 'I don't know what we were expecting, but we weren't expecting that!'

The evening was a great success, not least because of Marc. We didn't know it then, but this man was about to become a huge part of our lives and a close friend. I've enjoyed many jaunts with him to New York and his family's holiday home in the South of France. Apart from being brilliant at his job, he has the timing of a stand-up comedian, regaling us with impressions of everything, from naff boyband dance routines to bird, dolphin and cat noises. Marc had us weeping on every journey we took with him over several projects we worked on together. He asked us to play at the opening night of the Hard Rock in Dubai, which was a spectacular event. Afterwards, we were treated to a mini-holiday, complete with camel rides, high-speed desert safari trip, a desert storm that tore everything up, and an Eagles concert in the desert. In 2012, the Hard Rock asked us to play an eight-date US tour for their Pinktober breast cancer event, to which we happily agreed. It was great to get back on the road in America and fit in a bit of TV promo, appearing on WWHL with Andy Cohen and a breakfast TV show with Arnold Schwarzenegger.

—

KEREN: I've always loved the Olympics, but for some reason turned down the opportunity to go to the London opening ceremony in 2012 because I'd just got back to Cornwall after a stint away, and couldn't be bothered to head back to London. What was I thinking?

I watched it on TV, knowing Sara was in the crowd and bitterly regretting not being there. As a consolation, Andrew and I secured some tickets for the athletics and duly went to watch and soak up the atmosphere, draped in union flags.

Sara and I were thrilled to perform at Horse Guards Parade for the final of the beach volleyball. I've always loved that part of London, and have occasionally chanced upon the Trooping of the Colour, drawn in by the spectacle and ceremony.

After a rehearsal in the afternoon, we popped off to a hotel room to prepare and get our nails painted – red, white and blue, of course – before heading back. The transformation of the parade ground was amazing; the lights and banks of seating all around us against the night sky. It felt like an old amphitheatre, back in Verona, where we'd performed in the eighties. The crowd was deafening as we sang and danced on our podium, surrounded by a troupe of dancers. We could have happily stayed there all night.

I love it when the entire country gets swept up in a wave of emotion and patriotism – as did George Michael, who, of course, threw a fabulous Olympics party. Any excuse! It was one of the last big parties he had at his Highgate house with the usual extravagant catering and it was packed with celebs and new neighbours like Kate Moss.

In September 2012, we flew to Singapore to perform at the Grand Prix. Despite being put up in luxurious suites overlooking the racetrack, we moaned continually about the bloody racket of the cars. It was only when my son called and pointed out that he would have given anything to be in our shoes, I realised (a) how privileged I was, and (b) that I should've brought Tom along with me. We could see the massive stage from our balconies. But in order to get there, we had to negotiate all sorts of security, including being sealed into a car with tape, while driving such a circuitous route that a short journey 'across the road' took about an hour. When we arrived backstage, everyone was watching the race and of course, we went through our usual routine of: 'It's completely empty', 'What if nobody turns up?' and the old favourite, 'Is this really our audience?' We needn't have worried. In the end, we had around 50,000 people, all singing and waving their arms. I don't think we'll ever shake that anxiety we get before big shows, but then again maybe it's a good thing not to get complacent.

18
EVERY SUMMER HAS A STORY

KEREN: I've loved watching our kids grow up. When they were little, the five-year gap between Tom and Alice seemed vast, and back then, Tom was very much the big brother figure. I'm not sure when but at a certain point the noticeable gap wasn't there any more and, in some ways, perhaps because they aren't related, it has meant they can talk more openly with each other.

The holidays we've taken together to America, Barcelona, Rome and Venice have been some of my happiest times. We all share an interest in history, art and architecture, though I have to say Tom and Alice know a lot more than me. Alice studied history and has a degree in history of art, and Tom has a very impressive knowledge of history, although his degree was in film and TV production. On our trips, we combine visits to the beach and lazy lunches with visits to galleries and historical sites. Even though Sara and I have usually been to all these places before, going with the kids is always a new experience that casts them in a different light.

Casa Batllo in Barcelona.

In Barcelona, we visited the fantastic Gaudi buildings, but it was when we got to Rome that Tom was in his element. It was like having my own personal, talking guide book. For the first time, I'd booked an Airbnb, just off Piazza Navona. It looked terrific and was advertised as being suitable for six – so plenty of space for four, surely! Unfortunately not. It had one living/bedroom space with two double beds, which Sara, Alice and I shared, while Tom had a tiny spot with a mattress. The ladder that accessed this cramped space from the kitchen had to be removed in order to use the kitchen door. Rome was basking in a heatwave, and consequently, it was suffocating. Poor Tom always drew the short straw on his travels with us. Girls' privileges always came first! At least in Rome, when us girls decided to go shopping, he had the option of cramming in an extra visit to some tomb or other that grabbed his interest.

Alice told us she'd recently discovered Aperol Spritz and wanted to treat us to drinks, but we all hated it, including Alice herself. She made Tom buy her a rose from a street vendor, just to embarrass him. A feat I haven't managed since he was about thirteen and I asked him, in front of his friends, if he had pubic hair.

We were amused to note that on several occasions, Alice used Tom as a shield, pretending he was her boyfriend to deflect the amorous advances of unwanted Italian men, particularly when the two of them went off clubbing together. Of course, if she deemed her suitor attractive enough, she pretended not to know him, at least for the duration of a dance or two. Sara and I like to think we can still turn the odd head if we put in the effort, but when you throw a young, beautiful girl like Alice into the mix, the stark reality of the situation hits you head-on.

Venice may well be my favourite place in the world. Again, it was a place Sara and I had been, along with Jacquie, in the early nineties Bananarama days, but that time we were there with Radio 1 and although we did fit in a sneaky gondolier ride, it was very much a working trip.

This time, we arrived by train, and travelled up the Grand Canal to a rather more successful Airbnb, right by the Rialto Bridge. The Biennale was on and we spent a whole day there. We took the water bus to the lido and lounged around on the beach. We explored the alleyways for out-of-the-way bars and restaurants and danced around St Mark's Square to the orchestra like stereotypical tourists.

—

SARA: During a busy 2013, Keren and I downed tools and invited Tom and Alice on a four-week holiday to the USA. We'd been on plenty of family holidays together when they were young: everything from barbecues and games of rounders on Cornwall's beaches to five-star luxury hotels in Mauritius – but now they were in their late teens and early twenties. Yes, it had finally happened: our babies were young adults!

Our first stop was LA. We stayed at our friend Oliver's stunning house on Mulholland Drive, which has a wrap-around veranda offering the most spectacular views of the Hollywood Hills. Each morning, we'd breakfast outside, taking in the beautiful vista, listening to the birds and planning our day to a soundtrack of Lana Del Rey's 'Summertime Sadness', the Cedric Gervais remix.

Our kids are amazing and we've always been really close, but this holiday was special. They had grown up and were starting to make their own way in the world – Alice as a singer/songwriter and Tom as a film producer – so there was a sense that we might never do this again, just the four of us.

We hung out on the beaches in Santa Monica, Venice and Malibu. We rummaged around vintage stores; hired bikes and cycled along the boardwalk while Tom decided to rollerblade. He played ice-hockey at home, so took off confidently and at high speed, but less than five minutes in came clattering down on the concrete, damaging his shoulder. Our collective response, not for the first time, was 'Stop showing off, Tom!' which, over the years, has become a bit of a catchphrase.

Poor Tom. He takes it all in good spirits, but hanging out with three women at times must drive him nuts, especially when we're getting ready for a night out. Keren, Alice and I would monopolise the enormous bathroom for a good two hours, taking it in turns to shower and get ready, jostling at the mirrors, swapping hair straighteners, stopping intermittently to pour aperitifs or engage in girly chats. As soon as we were ready and waiting to head out, Keren would demand to know how long Tom was going to be, generously affording him five minutes before we ordered an Uber. He was always ready in time, bless him.

We had dinner with friends at the Chateau Marmont, met up with Siobhan and her kids to go clubbing, and shopped on Melrose Avenue and Robertson Boulevard before checking out the Walk of Fame on Hollywood Boulevard.

There, a young man dressed as Shrek spotted Alice and made a beeline for her, whisking her up in the air and spinning her around. She was mortified, not least because she was wearing a very short skirt. Once Shrek had placed Alice back on the star-studded pavement, he posed for a photo, which we hadn't ask for, and promptly tried to charge us $25 for the privilege. When we declined to cough up, Shrek became very shirty, his Hollywood smile evaporating. Deciding he was only trying to make a living, we ended up paying him, but if he'd have picked either Keren or me up and swung us around in the middle of Hollywood Boulevard, he mightn't have been as happy with the outcome – ogre or not!

After evenings out, we'd return home and sit out on the veranda for a nightcap under the stars, talking late into the night accompanied by a chorus of cicadas. We drank a lot of red wine, discussed relationships, our hopes and dreams, put the world to rights, and laughed hysterically.

In Vegas, we went horse riding at dusk through Red Rock Canyon in the Mojave Desert, taking in the vast mountain range. Watching the sunset over the Joshua trees made us feel like we were in a real-life western – it was awesome. Travelling back in the pitch-black was slightly less enjoyable, with my horse skidding down the mountain and rocks flying everywhere. On seeing my distress, the cowboy leading our posse turned to me and said, 'Don't worry, ma'am, the horse has four legs.' Which, I imagine, was meant to be reassuring. Meanwhile, somewhere in the distance, the air rang with the sound of Keren's screams, as her horse thrashed her under a spiky tree, cutting her face.

Back on solid ground, we were treated to a hearty, home-cooked meal, ruined only by the fact that there were no beers on hand, and that the trip leaders had forgotten to pack the marshmallows that we were hoping to toast over a fire. Still, keen not to let the lack of sugar and gelatine confectionery spoil our Wild-West experience, Keren and I made our way to the fire anyway, perking up somewhat when the cowboys whipped out their guitars for a singalong. No sooner had the opening chords of 'Take Me Home, Country Roads' twanged out into the smoky night air than Keren, Alice, Tom and I were off in full and fine voice.

After our very own version of *City Slickers*, we returned to the Bellagio and the kids headed to the club downstairs – The Bank. Keren and I told them we'd just have a nightcap and see them in the morning, so we ordered a glass of wine, settling back in our comfy bar chairs.

'Let's have one more,' I suggested as our glasses drained.

'Why not? We're on holiday,' Keren said.

The 'one more nightcap' malarkey continued late into the evening, intermittently interrupted by men with all sorts of terrible chat-up lines.

'You look as though you've just got off a horse,' one guy said, taking in our casual jeans and T-shirt attire.

Well, at least that one was original.

Tom and Alice were heading back to their rooms at around 4 a.m. when they spotted us in the still crowded bar and burst out laughing. I suspect that if they hadn't extricated us and taken us back to our rooms, we'd still have been there at breakfast time. We'd had a lovely evening, but the continuing mantra of 'let's just have one more' had meant that we'd been drinking wine by the glass instead of buying a bottle. This, of course, resulted in an extortionate bar bill.

The final destination on our American odyssey was

New York City, where we met up with a bunch of Alice's uni friends who were studying there. Keren and I partied with them briefly before leaving them to their own devices in a rooftop jacuzzi at a club night in the Standard Hotel, while we found alternative amusement at the legendary Marie's Crisis piano bar in Greenwich Village. There we drank dirt-cheap cocktails, while the resident pianist hammered out various Broadway classics and the assembled crowd of actors, theatre people, locals and tourists sang along with gusto.

It was a special trip and I consider myself lucky to have such a beautiful daughter, who's both a best friend and a confidante. Sounds like a line from *The Golden Girls* theme! She's an incredibly kind and thoughtful person and an excellent sounding board. I love her with all my heart, and Tommy too.

—

KEREN: They're similar in many ways, Tom and Alice; enormous fun to spend time with, but also thoughtful and sensitive. I can talk to either of them in a way I could never have spoken to my parents. I don't think Tom and I have ever had a phone conversation that didn't finish with 'I love you', even when he was on the school bus with his mates and I could hear them laughing in the background. We've helped each other get through some challenging times, and I'm hugely proud of the person he is. That goes for Alice too, who is a talented songwriter and whose beautiful voice moves me to tears.

—

SARA: Alice has always been as passionate about music as I am. From an early age, she'd take lead solo vocals in school musicals and plays and, although she was shy, she came into her own when acting and singing. She started writing songs when she was about ten and as we had a basic studio set up at home, her dad would record her vocals. I was aware that she had a great voice, but it wasn't until a school jazz concert, when she performed her version of Lady Gaga's 'Paparazzi' with a friend accompanying her on piano, that I realised just how good she was. At the end of the song, Alice got a standing ovation, and I was completely blown away.

Alice continued to write throughout her school days, and her musical achievements are entirely her own. Now she works in social media, which has supplemented the recordings of her two self-funded EPs, *Narcissus* and *Lioness*, which are a fusion of pop, dance and R&B. Her lyrics are thought-provoking and honest and have a real maturity to them. Recently I've written a couple of tracks with her just to see how we work together, and it was so natural and enjoyable, each of us bringing our own experiences to the table.

—

KEREN: The freedom to make our own choices in life is something Sara and I have passed on to our kids. As clichéd as it sounds, we just want them to be happy.

19

'CHANGE IS THE ONLY CONSTANT IN LIFE'

HERACLITUS

KEREN: Ageing is the classic double-edged sword. It gives you some pretty good stuff with one hand while swiftly pulling the rug from under you with the other.

At some point in my forties, I reached a point where I thought I had it all pretty much sorted. I felt comfortable, confident even, with the notion of getting older, and, yes, I liked myself. I'd also reflected on past experiences, good and bad, and decided that rather than being a repeat offender, it was finally time to learn from the many mistakes I had made. It may not have all been good, but it was mostly good, and what wasn't perfect was at least getting there.

So there you are: sorted, calm, content. Little did I know what sort of gigantic spanner Mother Nature was preparing to chuck into my almost perfectly balanced works.

OK, so I knew that at some point, being female, I

would have to deal with that thing called the menopause, but WTF! Call me naïve, but I'd been expecting a few hot flushes and the odd grey hair, but mostly wondered what the fuss was about. Christ, what did perimenopausal even mean? I'd never heard of it. Apparently, it's nature's way of easing you in, or, as I now see it, dragging it out for as long as humanly possible.

Before I knew what was happening, I found myself on what Sara and I both dubbed the 'Tubby Australian Tour'. Suddenly, my clothes were uncomfortably tight around the waist. Indeed, both of us found ourselves resorting to the more flattering bell-shaped tops. I was horrified to notice, while sitting in front of a make-up mirror, preparing for a show, that my already dangerously fragile hairline had developed even more discernible gaps. What the hell was going on? I completely freaked out at first, but after several blood tests and a visit to a trichologist who told me that thinning hair was typical at my age, I accepted it. Sod it, I thought, if it gets any worse, I'll just wear a hat. Or a wig. Or both.

—

SARA: The older I get, the more I realise how lucky I am to have had this lifelong friendship with Keren. I'm conscious as I write this of how many times I've mentioned how much we laugh, but it's the absolute backbone of our friendship. We are there for one another through thick and thin, through every change in our lives and that includes the delights of the menopause, the final frontier. We always try to see the funny side. Of

263

course, there's nothing funny about insomnia, anxiety or mental fatigue to name but a few symptoms, but laughing about not being able to get your top done up before going on stage, your shoes being too tight or your hair taking a turn for the worse is what gets us through it. It shocks me that up until quite recently it was still such a taboo subject.

—

KEREN: I think the worst thing of all was the mental fuzz, diminishing my ability to focus or cope with almost anything that was going on around me. This started with a terrible three- or four-year period in which my dad, who had been incredibly active all his life, had a heart attack followed by two strokes. Up until then, he'd been caring for my mum whose mental state had deteriorated over the years along with her physical health due to an inherited lung condition, despite being a non-smoker. When he died, my brother and I had to take over looking after Mum. On top of all that, my beautiful cousin Helen became very ill with cancer. She was the same age as me, and we had grown up together. Helen had recently bought a house in Cornwall in the hope of spending more time there. During her illness, she put all her efforts into her family and created some very special memories for us all, handling the whole thing bravely and brilliantly.

I guess you could say that 2016 was my annus horribilis. In the space of two months, I lost a dear friend, my mum, my auntie, and my cousin Helen. I've often felt guilty that so many terrible things have happened to people around me while I, in many ways, seem to have lived a sort of charmed existence. I've drunk, I've smoked, I eat loads of sugar, yet I seem to stay healthy. In fact, besides the Tubby Australian tour, I don't even put on weight. Even when I was younger, I always felt like I was the lucky one. My brother Matt was in a horrific motorbike accident at the age of eighteen. His bike went under a van, putting him in a coma for several weeks. I was twenty-one at the time, and when it looked like he might need care for the rest of his life, I was ready to leave London to go home and help look after him. Fortunately, it never came to that, but he was consequently diagnosed with MS, which was a terrible blow. Matt has handled the challenges of living with MS with a huge amount of determination and dignity, working for as long as possible to support his boys, George, Harry and Jack, along with his wife, Helen. I'm very proud of him, and I always enjoy spotting his beaming face in the crowd at our shows, knowing he's proud of me too.

At the end of that year, Tom and I were at the home of my cousin Helen's family, enjoying Christmas Day together. It was wonderful to be there with her sister, husband and children, but also incredibly hard having lost her to cancer in September. At some point in the day my phone rang. It was Andrew, who called to tell me that George was dead. Aside from the terrible shock, it seemed unbearably painful coming on top of everything else.

I stayed in the garden for a while, had a bit of a cry, then went back inside to be with the family and carry on the evening. I didn't know what else I could do. Helen's family had been through so much, and I didn't want to make it all about me and my sadness when they were trying so hard to have a lovely Christmas Day. Since then, Helen's daughter, Sarah, has become an even more significant part of my life. She'd already spent a few summers with me in Cornwall, but since her mother's death we've become very close, and I like to think the bond we have has helped us both through some sorrowful times.

It's funny, the way that pain and loss can have unexpected consequences, and at the start of 2017, I felt strangely positive; determined to make the most of life going forward.

20
THE REUNION

SARA: In 2016, while flying back from touring Australia and Japan, Keren and I discussed what we might do the following year. We were already talking about recording a new album, but we were looking for a new project of some kind, something different, challenging and exciting.

We decided to speak to our friend Peter Loraine about the possibility of him managing us, curious to see what ideas he might have. After leaving him to think about it for a couple of weeks, he had a conversation with Keren.

'This is probably not what you had in mind,' he said, 'but I think you should do a reunion tour with Siobhan.' He was right, that definitely wasn't on our radar.

We'd seen Siobhan sporadically over the years. One of the most recent times had been in LA in 2013. We'd had dinner at Ceccone's in West Hollywood, followed by a rip-roaring night at Giorgio's – where we actually met the club's namesake, legendary record producer,

Giorgio Moroder. We also had a night out there with all our kids: Siobhan's two boys, Sam and Django, along with Tom and Alice. It was nice for Django and Alice to see each other again after so long, as they'd played together when they were little. As always, it had been great seeing Siobhan, with the wonderful camaraderie between the three of us still very much there.

That said, we weren't convinced by Peter's idea and it certainly hadn't been what we were expecting to hear. His thoughts were that Bananarama had only ever toured after Siobhan had left the group, so it was the one thing we hadn't managed to do together. This was true but was completely out of sync with our vision for the future of the band.

—

KEREN: On the one hand, the idea of the three original members of Bananarama reuniting to hit the road again was an exciting prospect. On the other hand, a project as big as this was bound to interrupt the recording and release of our new album. As well as that, we'd worked so incredibly hard to become a successful live act as a duo, that Sara and I wondered if touring as a trio, even as a one-off, would impact negatively on everything we'd achieved over the years.

—

SARA: Over the coming days, the more Keren and I discussed it, the more viable it seemed. Maybe it was the project we were looking for. A once-in-a-lifetime tour, a celebration of our time together. It could be fantastic. We certainly knew the fans would love a reunion, and an added bonus of having the original line-up on tour was that it would afford us the budget to create an amazing show, with all the bells and whistles.

In December, Keren and I called Siobhan for a FaceTime chat to ask if she was interested. The idea came as a complete shock to her as well. We left it on the table over Christmas, giving us all time to mull it over.

—

KEREN: Siobhan was reticent about the idea of a reunion tour for different reasons. She hadn't performed live for quite some time, and the only live show she'd played with Sara and me was one song at G-A-Y in London, for our twentieth anniversary in 2002.

When she flew over from LA to discuss the idea further, however, it felt like a long-lost sister had returned to the fold. We spoke about how amazing it felt to perform our songs with thousands of people singing along. And after all the sorrow of 2016, I was very aware of wanting to do something different and not wanting to miss any new opportunities. In the end, we all decided we had to go for it.

—

SARA: We knew we were in safe hands with Peter, who negotiated a deal with Steve Homer at the tour promoters, AEG. By January, it was all systems go and we announced the tour on Graham Norton's TV show, where we joined

Margot Robbie, Harrison Ford, Ryan Gosling and Reese Witherspoon on the sofa for a quick chat. With that, the initial eighteen shows sold out immediately, so another eight dates were added, which also sold out fast.

We were blessed with a fantastic team, which included Rob Sinclair, who designed the incredible stage sets. Aside from our trusty band, J Boy, Simon, Adam and Rich, we had our old friend Steve Levitt on production, Alice taking the helm on social media, her boyfriend, Nick Dynan, designing the tour programme, and a great promo team. The finishing touches were the amazing costumes, which were distinctly space-age rock 'n' roll! Meanwhile, preparing the setlist and sifting through old unseen video footage and photographs for the video-screen element of the show reminded us of all the good things we'd done together.

—

KEREN: Sara and I were keen to use our established musicians for the tour along with a new Musical Director, Richard Taylor. Bananarama already had a brilliant and talented touring band, so there was no need for a change of personnel as far as we were concerned. I'm not sure Siobhan was overly happy using only our people at first, but we knew just how good they were, and besides, they knew half the set already.

Sara and I would've needed a few rehearsals, but for Siobhan, there was so much to learn. To help her out, I filmed myself at home, doing some of the dance routines, then emailed the footage over to her while she was in LA. That way, she had a bit of homework to do before she came to London, giving her the chance to catch up a bit, at least with all the moves. Meanwhile, Sara and I cracked on with Ian Masterson, who created brilliant new arrangements for the songs.

With this new set-up involving the three of us, we were conscious that the show had to have more structure, so we drafted in a choreographer, our old friend Nathan Clark, plus Adrian Gas to get the staging right as well as the dance routines. As it turned out, when it came to the performances we probably took out more moves than we left in, as we wanted to have fun on stage rather than concentrating on what we were supposed to be doing next the whole time. We worked on our stage costume designs with Aldene Johnson, and each time she brought them into the rehearsal studio for a fitting, the excitement and reality of what we were about to do bubbled to the surface.

—

SARA: During the first few days of rehearsal, we all found ourselves getting quite emotional, tearful even, at hearing and performing some of the songs from the early days. The melancholy lyrics to 'Cheers Then' really got us all going.

Before we knew it, the opening night of the tour, at Belfast SSE Arena, was upon us. It was an incredible moment, standing excitedly on the top of a glossy black staircase, three little silhouettes behind a gauze, waiting for it to drop for our reveal.

Siobhan was so nervous and I felt very protective of her while we were on stage. I wanted this to be a good experience and for her to enjoy it as much as I hoped to. She was great and got into the swing of things pretty quickly and a few shows in, we were all having an absolute ball.

Keren and I had thought it would be nice to include 'Stay' – Siobhan's most famous Shakespears Sister hit – in the set. She wasn't sure it would work, but we rehearsed it, and it sounded great – I think we did it justice. It made for a poignant moment in the show, with the three of us walking up the stairs towards a backdrop of the moon. In turn, Siobhan loved our song 'Preacher Man' from the *Pop Life* album, so we added that to the set too. Another highlight was performing our very first single, the Swahili classic 'Aie a Mwana'. The screens were just so vibrant,

but the performance left us totally out of breath, as we darted from one side of the stage to the other. The encore of 'It Ain't What You Do' was great with its inspired 1920s swing arrangement with dance moves to match. Appearing at the top of the stairs with our backs to the audience, we revealed sequinned jackets with the initials of our names emblazoned across the back.

—

KEREN: I was surprised at how different it felt performing with two other people instead of just one. With two of us on stage, I barely had to think about anything, apart from enjoying myself. Everything just seemed to fall into place, and it all came naturally. Sara and I were almost telepathic in our movements; having become so accustomed to working as a duo for twenty-six years, our stage routine was practically second nature. We'd drop in and out of choreography quite naturally, and I always knew which harmony Sara was going to go to on a song, so I would typically go to another. Suddenly there was another person to consider, to bring into the fold, and the first few shows with Siobhan felt very different. I was acutely aware that this was a relatively alien experience for her. I didn't want her to feel like Sara and I were off and running, doing our own thing, while leaving her out on a limb, so if she moved to the front or side of the stage, I mirrored her. In the end, I needn't have worried about Siobhan at all; she performed with boundless energy and enthusiasm. After all, that's what we were always about, rather than some polished stage-school act.

Despite all the fun we had on stage, there was the odd thing about working with Siobhan that I hadn't missed. Her tardiness, which always drove me mad. We often found ourselves waiting on the tour bus while she farted around in the services. Sometimes, she drifted around to the point that I felt like attaching toddler reins to her to guide her around. It was frustrating, but we just had to laugh about it. This had always been Siobhan's way, and we simply had to get used to it again.

—

SARA: My mum and my sister Lindsey came to a few of the shows; I spotted them as soon as I stepped on stage. They were on their feet and singing along throughout the show. They enjoyed meeting Siobhan and her sister Maire backstage, telling me that the two of them felt like family. Keren's brother Matt and his sons were present and very proud too. Alice loved the tour bus experience and did the most brilliant job capturing the behind-the-scenes moments for our live DVD and some stills for the accompanying book.

If there is one moment that crystallises the joy of our friendship with Siobhan, it was on the tour bus one night heading home along the M6. It was gone midnight, and we'd been driving for a few hours when we suddenly ground to a halt behind a never-ending queue of stationary cars. The motorway was closed! What to do? There were two bottles of red wine, but no glasses. So, thinking on our feet, we grabbed a couple of empty Evian bottles and a bread knife and fashioned our own. Toasting our success, we chanced upon an old song – a childhood favourite from the 1970s – on Spotify. With that, we all burst into a raucous rendition of 'Those Were the Days' by Mary Hopkin. Siobhan got carried away and came in with the chorus too soon, her voice cracking from tiredness, while Keren pretended to play the tuba. Within minutes, we were all rolling around with laughter, and whenever I catch sight of the resulting video clip on Instagram, it makes me smile.

—

KEREN: So much of the rehearsal time and the tour was filled with unbridled laughter and joy. Siobhan is naturally comedic. She is prone to making wild, sweeping statements in a way I can't imagine anyone else doing, and I'd missed that.

During a break in rehearsals, I went down to Kent to spend the weekend with Siobhan, her sister Maire and Maire's partner Victoria, who is Chris Lowe of the Pet Shop Boys' sister. We drank copious amounts of wine, and the photos from the evening sum everything up, with Siobhan and I hugging and hysterically guffawing. Sara and I had always loved spending time with Maire. Back in the day, she was on a promo trip to the US with us, and Siobhan always introduced her in the same way.

'This is my sister, Maire, you might recognise her as Eileen from the "Come On Eileen" video.'

It's true, though I think she got a little tired of Siobhan's constant reminder.

SARA: Peter, Steve Homer and the team did an amazing job and the tour was a triumph. We got rave reviews, maximum media coverage and the audiences were sensational. I just remember looking out at everyone on their feet, dancing and singing with smiles on their faces, night after night. It really was a joyous experience.

There were also some unforgettable moments after the tour, such as being asked to perform at the Sonia Rykiel fashion show to close Paris Fashion Week. We arrived the day before and went to her store, where they dressed us for the show. Best of all was the models walking out in the finale to Bananarama songs. We also played a handful of sold-out dates in America and Canada.

When I think of Bananarama now, it's as a duo, and it's been that way for a long time, in fact twenty-eight years. Although our lives and careers have moved on, there is still a bond between Siobhan, Keren and me like no other. There's the sense of humour we all share, and during the tour I remembered how it felt when it was the three of us against the world, striving to be heard and appreciated as young women in a male-dominated business. I thought about that nervous first performance on *Top of the Pops* with Fun Boy Three, performing on *American Bandstand*, getting into scrapes with Duran Duran in Germany, Band Aid, the excitement of 'Cruel Summer' hitting the Top Ten in America, filming the video for it in NYC, and the excitement when 'Venus' became number one. So many memories.

We had some wonderful late-night talks on the tour

bus, plus the obligatory impromptu, out-of-control, on-board discos with the band, and the odd raucous singalong. These were the moments with Siobhan that I'd missed. All in all, the reunion tour was a wonderful, nostalgic trip, full of laughs and great memories.

—

KEREN: Throughout the tour, I had a few discussions with Siobhan about the past, the dynamic of the band back in the day, and, of course, the break-up. Not things we probably would have discussed had we not been in close quarters again for a sustained amount of time, but here we were. The thing that struck me was that Siobhan's perception of what had happened was in stark contrast to mine. She has her version of history, which is different from the one Sara and I remember. I don't think that will ever change, and I don't think it matters any more.

I think perhaps some people were expecting the three of us to record an album together, but that had never been the plan, although we did try to write and record a single together. For me, and for Peter, the single didn't work. It just wasn't good enough. Had we had more time, maybe we could have come up with something better, but we were so busy with everything else that it never happened. As well as that, Sara and I had already started recording our new album with Ian. Now we intended to get back into the studio and finish it. The tour was over, and it was back to business as a duo, but it had been a magnificent interlude!

21

FULL CIRCLE

KEREN: At the end of January 2019, we performed in LA at the Microsoft Theatre with The Bangles and OMD, followed by a solo show at The Observatory in Orange County. To keep things running seamlessly between acts at the LA show, the theatre used a revolving stage. Out of view of the audience, we set up while another artist was playing. When their set finished, our band struck up the intro to our first song, and the stage spun around, revealing us to the audience. This might have been marvellously efficient, but unfortunately, on the way round, my in-ear monitors stopped working. Changing them at this point was impossible, and as we moved into position, I was horrified to see a massive timer counting us down at the front of the stage. It was there to time our performance to the very second, making sure we didn't run over our allotted stage-time. It was terrifying.

The San Diego show was something else. A packed-out, standing-only theatre with a fantastic atmosphere. In between songs, the show turned into an impromptu

Bumped into the lovely Tony Swain at Kew Gardens, 2019.

On our tour in Australia, 2019.

Q&A session, which was hilarious, plus a good indication that we'd enjoy our upcoming album launch shows, for which we'd planned full audience Q&As.

Before that, however, we had another tour of Australia to complete. We'd played there a few years before, after a gap of about fifteen years. We'd have probably gone out more often, but we both hated the long flights and the resulting jet lag. Neither of us ever manage to sleep on flights, even on a flat bed. I always imagine a bucket of red wine will help, but it never does, even with an accompanying sleeping pill. The nearest I got to full relaxation on a flight was when someone gave me a Diazepam one time. I didn't sleep, but at the same time, I didn't give a shit what happened. Usually, any sign of turbulence sends us both into a panic, but on that flight, nothing fazed me.

On our previous Australian tour, we'd found ourselves flying backwards and forwards between time zones, so this time we decided to be more methodical, starting on one coast and finishing on the other. Stupidly, we started on the west coast and flew east, meaning we lost time as we travelled, so still ended up completely exhausted. We had no time off until we got to Sydney, where we kicked back and met up with friends and family. Now we could put on our bikinis and head to the beach. Only we didn't, deciding at the last minute that bikinis and beaches probably weren't a good idea after all. Why? Well, because I have an abject fear of being spotted by the press and being photographed in an unflattering light, which these days, quite frankly, is any light.

I still love touring. It means not having to think or plan your day, as each morning I get a piece of paper pushed under my hotel door with an itinerary. Every day in Australia we had an office hour in my room, where we went through emails while I lay on the bed in one of my five-euro Greek kaftans. After all these years on the road, Sara and I still spend a lot of time in one another's rooms, lounging around, chatting and eating.

I'm sure that to some of the staff who come in to deliver room service, it must look like we're a couple. One member of the band recently said to me that they can always tell when we're nearby because of the continuous howls of laughter. Well, either that or they can hear us complaining about something.

Sometime during January 2019, we received an email from Paul Franklin at CAA with an offer to play the Avalon Stage at Glastonbury. A week later, when we hadn't replied, he followed up with another, more urgent email. It wasn't that we didn't want to discuss it, we just weren't sure we wanted to do it. True, playing Glasto comes with a certain amount of kudos and it would be another tick in the box of things we hadn't yet done, but the thing was, we'd already had an offer to headline at another festival on the same weekend.

When we emailed back to say we weren't sure if we'd do it, Paul was horrified and hastily organised a conference call between the three of us and our other agent, Chris Ibbs.

'I have to say, girls, that I've never informed an artist of a slot – any slot – at Glastonbury without them jumping for joy,' Paul said.

Jumping for joy was never something we were prone to do even in our younger days, so we were hardly about to start now.

Paul persevered. 'Trust me on this one, you will love it.'

Unusually for us, we listened, finally agreeing to do it.

Five months later, there we were, held captive in a

holding pen in the Glastonbury car park because we didn't have the correct passes.

'I knew we shouldn't have done this,' I joked to Sara. 'They won't even let us in.'

—

SARA: Finally liberated from the car park, we set off through the vast festival grounds. It was a glorious, hot summer day and we soaked up the atmosphere as we passed the themed stages, patchwork fields of tents, eateries, and people basking in the sunshine. Everyone looked really happy and chilled.

I wasn't nervous about our performance – we'd been playing live now for more than twenty years – but I was a bit anxious about what kind of audience awaited us. On our arrival at the backstage area the place was pretty empty and that included the tent we were going to be performing in. We decided to grab some lunch and as we walked around the hospitality area people were stopping us for selfies and several festival goers said that there had been a real buzz over the weekend about us playing. That was good to hear and, as our stage time approached, we could see a surge of people, like migrating wildebeest, beating a path to our tent.

—

KEREN: From backstage, the place sounded like it was buzzing, and when we finally hit the stage, we realised just how packed it was. The tent walls were dragged completely open, and the crowd stretched as far as the eye could see. It was an incredible sight to behold. During the first song, my in-ear monitors conked out. I got the battery pack swapped over, but they still weren't working, so in the end, I did it old-school, using just the front-of-stage monitors. We started our show with one of our biggest hits, 'I Heard a Rumour', and then powered through a set of hits spanning our thirty-seven years together as Bananarama. The entire experience was amazing, and I could see Paul, standing stage right, beaming a smile. Thrilled, I'd imagine, to have been proved right.

—

SARA: There was a sea of hands in the air and everybody was singing along, which never fails to move me. I

Interview after our performance at BBC Radio 2 Live in Hyde Park.

283

literally couldn't have been happier. It was a wonderful, uplifting experience, and all the trepidation I'd felt about the audience seemed like a very distant memory.

Towards the end of the set, some of the BBC outside broadcast team were dispatched to catch a few moments of our show and interview us when we came off stage, and, still buzzing from the show, it was time for a well-deserved, celebratory gin and tonic.

—

KEREN: When we came off stage, still hugely energised from our performance and the reception we'd received, somebody told us that during our set, security had been forced shut the gates because too many people had tried to get in and it was getting dangerous. Crikey, not

Signing copies of our album *In Stereo*, 2019.

only were we a hit at Glastonbury, we were a health and safety issue!

—

SARA: Along with Ian Masterson, we'd been writing songs for our next album, *In Stereo*, for a couple of years. While none of us was entirely sure how, when or where this would be released, we continued, undeterred. It had been ten years since our album *Viva* was released, through Universal Music. We'd released some EPs and singles in that time, but had mostly concentrated on touring. Putting out music in the current climate, however, was much easier. Gone were the days of racking up hundreds of thousands of pounds on studio time to record an album. Everybody had a home studio now and could put an album together for a fraction of the price. So, for those artists who didn't have the multimillion-pound record deals, self-funding was the route du jour.

Keren and I discussed the realities of self-release, financial and otherwise, with Ian, ultimately deciding to go for it.

The plan was to write and record all the music, mix and master the album, then put the photoshoot, artwork and social media together with the help of Alice and her talented young friends, creative director Nell Campbell and photographer Will Marsh. We delivered the finished album to a label services company called Absolute, who licensed and distributed it. Together, we assembled an excellent promo team, most of whom we'd worked with in the past. Logistically, it was hard work. Essentially, Keren and I were our own record company and management. For us, though, it turned out to be the perfect way to operate, leaving us in complete control of the product and its exploitation and retaining full ownership of our music.

Right from the start, it felt right. The first single, 'Stuff Like That', was A-listed on the playlists and then made record of the week on BBC Radio 2. The video was shot by Andy Morahan. We'd bumped into Andy, who'd directed videos for some of our big hits in the past, after a meeting at the Groucho Club. His first words to us were, 'When are we going to work together again?'

'Funny you should say that,' we chorused. It was pure fate!

The second single, 'Looking for Someone', was also

Graham Norton, BBC Radio 2.

A-listed. Now we were geared up and ready to start our album launch tour. We'd discussed playing a handful of intimate venues with Paul Franklin and Chris Ibbs from CAA, with the idea of starting the show with a thirty-minute Q&A, followed by a live set consisting of the new album and some never-before-performed tracks from our duo albums. Some of our own favourite songs! In no time, Steve Homer from AEG was on board and loved the idea.

—

KEREN: For once, I even enjoyed the promo side of things, feeling more relaxed than I had done for years. In our Radio 2 interview with Graham Norton, we were laughing so much while he was playing the music, I had no idea what actually went out on the radio. The

rehearsals for the tour were also a lot of fun. We always love performing our classic hits, and there's no better feeling than hearing a huge crowd singing along with us, but this was something different. As we were performing to true fans, we could do whatever songs we wanted, including ones that we loved but had never played before.

—

SARA: The opening night of the tour was at the Omeara in London and the place was packed and jumping, with a sell-out crowd. We'd never done a Q&A before, so quite honestly didn't know whether we were going to fall flat on our faces or not. We didn't, thank goodness. In fact, after we'd run twenty minutes over, we had to be ushered off the stage so we could get ready for the live set. It was like a sauna in that room, but when we hit the stage, with the wind machines blasting, it was electric. I performed like I never had before and felt ecstatically happy. It was a mixture of delight at playing new material that I was immensely proud of, singing our personal favourites from the nineties, and looking at my best friend beside me, thinking, *look how far we've come together*. We played the Borderline the next night, followed by Glee club in Birmingham, Gorilla in Manchester and St Peter's in Glasgow. Each audience was as brilliant as the one before.

When our self-funded album charted, we were over the moon. The feedback we got from all quarters made me think, *wow, thirty-seven years on and people are still loving what we do.*

22

'A GOOD FRIEND KNOWS ALL YOUR BEST STORIES BUT A BEST FRIEND HAS LIVED THEM WITH YOU'

ANONYMOUS

KEREN: These days, I feel settled and happy most of the time. I've not been in a serious relationship for a few years, and I'm comfortable with that. In the past, maybe I've needed to be in love because the feel of it made me love myself a little more. Up until now, I'd never lived on my own, yet now I can't imagine living with somebody else, with all the compromise that entails.

I'm not perfect, but that's OK, just as long as I'm not hurting anyone else. Those are the only regrets I have; the times when my actions might have hurt others. Nowadays, family and friends are more important than ever. Sara and I are lucky enough to have reached a point where we can choose how much work we do. We still get a massive thrill out of Bananarama, particularly the live shows, and have no intention of giving it up any time soon. It's sometimes been a bit of a battle to keep our heads above water in what is undoubtedly a sexist and ageist business, but the experiences we've shared mean we have the confidence to keep moving forward in whatever way we see fit.

—

SARA: We've always strived to keep as much control as we could of our work, our output and our 'brand', and it's important to us that we have the final say. The Bananarama name is mine and Keren's trademark; we've built it up over a long career, so it's vital that people we work with understand and share our vision, because if something goes wrong, the buck stops with us. There's mutual respect between us and those we collaborate with musically, and those who are integral to the band's ongoing success, and we're incredibly grateful for what they bring.

Bananarama means everything to us from a creative standpoint, and it's our business. It grew from a germ of an idea in the eighties to where we are today. It's our baby, and for the most part, our intuitive way of working has stood us in good stead – and long may it continue!

Women always seem to be up against a ticking clock for one reason or another, but as Keren and I reach our fourth decade in the music industry, I think we've weathered most storms. Now that we're in our fifties we know what's important and what to let go of. I'm thankful for the wisdom age brings. I still enjoy writing songs, releasing music and touring but I also understand now the importance of a work/life balance and getting to enjoy the places we visit.

This is the only job I've ever had and I realise how fortunate I have been. I've also come out of the madness intact and, having written some of this book during a time of pandemic and lockdown, I have had time to reflect and really appreciate the simple things in life.

I appreciate our fans more than ever now; through social media you get to understand a little of how people feel about our music and what it means to them. Whether it's those who have accompanied us on our epic journey through the decades or those who have just enjoyed one or two of our songs, I am genuinely thankful. And the sheer embrace and love from the LGBTQ community throughout our career has been immense and hugely important to the group. We will always be grateful for that.

—

KEREN: I guess we've talked a fair bit about partying and nights out in this book, but that's when all the weird and wonderfully random encounters seem to happen to us. It certainly wasn't every night of the week, but it would be challenging to fill a book with, 'stayed in, cooked a meal, ate the meal, watched TV and went to bed'. Even though we spend many, many evenings doing just that when we're together (though not the going to bed bit, I should point out). When I go to London these days, I almost always stay at Sara's, and that's us! Even now, though, it's rarely dull, and still usually involves much guffawing, hilarity, impersonations of people from TV, and ridiculous dance moves in the kitchen. Yes, there are times when we discuss politics, religion and what's going on in the world. But more regularly these days we talk about how we're feeling personally and emotionally, which, in hindsight, was very much lacking in our younger years. It's funny, whenever we spot two old ladies laughing together, looking like they're having fun, one of us will remark, 'That'll be us!'

We'd always gravitated towards Soho, and have seen it go through many changes. These days, a lot of its magic is being eroded. In the eighties, seedy strip joints and thriving youth culture seemed to mix seamlessly, and it was a place where you didn't have to have money in order to soak up the buzz and the atmosphere. As spartan as our life was in those days, it was also very exciting, and I feel blessed to have had experiences that have shaped both my career and my character. I can't imagine teenagers these days being able to have a similar experience to the one Sara and I had. I know development and modernisation are inevitable, but it would be a shame to lose the last vestiges of character that Soho has managed to cling onto. Even now, I can't imagine not regularly going out in Soho, regardless of how much it changes.

—

SARA: Sometimes now, when we're performing on stage, I catch sight of Keren out of the corner of my eye, high kicking and having a ball, and I picture us at age thirteen, working out dance routines in her living room. We've come so far together. I'm so proud of the both of us. I have my family and friendships and I take nothing for granted and I am living my life my way.

—

KEREN: Siobhan once said to us, in one of her typically wild, sweeping statements, 'Your friendship is unnatural!' I found it funny. It seems to me like the most natural thing in the world. Maybe it's 'unusual' in the fact that it's still going strong after all these years, especially with all the ups and downs we have had both personally and professionally, but a life without Sara in it is one I can't possibly imagine.

ACKNOWLEDGEMENTS

I will be forever grateful to Keren for her friendship, love and laughter. And for Sara, my best friend through the joy and the tears, life would have been very dull without you!

Along with our beautiful children, Tom and Alice, we'd like to thank our families for their love and support.

Thank you to all the people we have worked with throughout our career and who have helped bring our vision to life. And to all the musicians, dancers and producers for their outstanding talent and hilarious company. For her belief in this memoir we'd like to thank the ever enthusiastic Jocasta Hamilton; Charlotte Bush, Director of Media and Public Relations; Laura Brooke, Publicity Director; Rebecca Ikin, Marketing Director; Henry Petrides, Senior Designer; Konrad Kirkham, Senior Production Manager; Anna Argenio, Editor; Rose Waddilove, Assistant Editor; Claire Simmonds, her sales team, and everyone else involved at Hutchinson, Penguin Random House. A special thank you to Terry Ronald, Tim Bates at PFD and Jon Fowler for their help in the realisation of this project. Forever grateful to Ian Masterson, Chris Organ and Pascal Maurice. Last but not least, Alice Dallin-Walker for her invaluable help with this memoir. Love you Bun!

Genuine thanks to our friends and of course to our fans.

IMAGE CREDITS